A Political Economy of Behavioural Public Policy

Behavioural public policy has thus far been dominated by approaches that are based on the premise that it is entirely legitimate for policy-makers to design policies that nudge or influence people to avoid desires that may not be in their own self- interest. This book argues, instead, for a liberal political economy that radically departs from these paternalistic frameworks. Oliver argues for a framework whereby those who impose no substantive harms on others ought to be free of manipulative or coercive interference. On this view, BPP does not seek to "correct" an individual's conception of the desired life. This book is the third in a trilogy of books by Adam Oliver on the origins and conceptual foundations of BPP.

ADAM OLIVER is a behavioural economist and behavioural public policy analyst in the Department of Social Policy at the London School of Economics and Political Science. He has published and taught widely in the areas of health economics and policy, behavioural economics and behavioural public policy. He is a founding editor-in-chief of the journals *Health Economics, Policy and Law* and *Behavioural Public Policy*. He edited *Behavioural Public Policy* (Cambridge University Press, 2013) and authored *The Origins of Behavioural Public Policy* (Cambridge University Press, 2017) and *Reciprocity and the Art of Behavioural Public Policy* (Cambridge University Press, 2019). He is the chair of the International Behavioural Public Policy Association and founder of the Annual International Behavioural Public Policy Conference.

A Political Economy of Behavioural Public Policy

ADAM OLIVER

London School of Economics and Political Science

CAMBRIDGE
UNIVERSITY PRESS

Shaftesbury Road, Cambridge CB2 8EA, United Kingdom

One Liberty Plaza, 20th Floor, New York, NY 10006, USA

477 Williamstown Road, Port Melbourne, VIC 3207, Australia

314–321, 3rd Floor, Plot 3, Splendor Forum, Jasola District Centre,
New Delhi – 110025, India

103 Penang Road, #05–06/07, Visioncrest Commercial, Singapore 238467

Cambridge University Press is part of Cambridge University Press & Assessment,
a department of the University of Cambridge.

We share the University's mission to contribute to society through the pursuit of
education, learning and research at the highest international levels of excellence.

www.cambridge.org
Information on this title: www.cambridge.org/9781009282567

DOI: 10.1017/9781009282574

First published 2023

A catalogue record for this publication is available from the British Library

ISBN 978-1-009-28256-7 Hardback
ISBN 978-1-009-28255-0 Paperback

For those who remain true to themselves

Contents

Illustrations

x

Preface

The book that you have before you is the third and thus final part of a trilogy that I have in recent years written on the development and, perhaps in part, future of the relatively new field of behavioural public policy. The book follows and builds upon *The Origins of Behavioural Public Policy* (Oliver, 2017) and *Reciprocity and the Art of Behavioural Public Policy* (Oliver, 2019), and the title – *A Political Economy of Behavioural Public Policy* – is inspired by John Stuart Mill's *Principles of Political Economy*.[1]

THEME

In 2019, Vladimir Putin, an embodiment of why liberalism is of such fundamental importance to humankind, proclaimed that liberalism is dead.[2] Putin, like Bismarck (and many others) before him (see Rosenblatt, 2018, p.193), seems to believe that oppression is required to hold a large state together, and thus celebrates liberalism's demise. Putin is wrong. Liberalism is not dead, but it is quite poorly, and it needs to be revived.

In this book, in the spirit of Mill – and of Wilhelm von Humboldt (1791–1792/1993), who influenced him greatly – I will argue for a political economy of behavioural public policy that is anti-paternalistic – that stands with the notion that the choices, actions and behaviours of those who are imposing no harms on others ought to be free of manipulative or coercive interference from third parties (and particularly from policy makers).[3] When externalities are not an issue, I contend that policy makers ought to limit themselves to protecting and nurturing the almost innate human tendencies to reciprocate and cooperate, for these tendencies have evolved to give each person the best chance of achieving their own conception of the desired life. As Mill (1848/1970, pp.313–314) noted:

[I]t is ... of supreme importance that all classes of the community, down to the lowest, should have much to do for themselves; that as great a demand should be made upon their intelligence and virtue as it is in any respect equal to; that the government should not only leave as far as possible to their own faculties the conduct of whatever concerns themselves alone, but should suffer them, or rather encourage them, to manage as many as possible of their joint concerns by voluntary co-operation; since this discussion and management of collective interests is the great school of that public spirit, and the great source of that intelligence of public affairs, which are always regarded as the distinctive character of the public of free countries.

Although this book espouses liberalism, it recognises quite forcefully that freedom without constraints offers a great deal of scope for the egoistically inclined to act upon their instincts, to the detriment of most of us. Mill likewise deplored egoism – 'the egotism which thinks self and its concerns more important than everything else, and decides all doubtful questions in its own favour; – these are moral vices, and constitute a bad and odious moral character' (Mill, 1859/1969, p.75) – and considered its expression legitimate grounds for government regulation if it imposed unreasonable harms on others.[4] Mill contended that where the threat of government punishment for harms imposed on others exists, people are to a degree freed from having to protect themselves, and thus their energies – as well as those of the would-be egoists – can be devoted to more fruitful, cooperative endeavours. In short, in order to protect freedom in general, some specific freedoms ought to be constrained, which is an important component of the political economy of behavioural public policy proposed in the following pages.

NOTES ON STYLE

Like my previous books, I have tried to write this one in a style that will be accessible and interesting to a multidisciplinary audience, and to experts, policy makers, students and interested laypersons. It is not, however, what is commonly known as a "trade book" (i.e. a popular science book). To get the most out of it, the reader must be prepared to put some work into it. The reader will be able to understand my arguments from the main text, but the endnotes included in all of the chapters provide digressions and enrich the narrative, which some readers may find appealing and instructive. At the end of each chapter, in the form of a few questions, I have provided some "Food for Thought". I, of course, hope that the whole book provides some intellectual nourishment.

Acknowledgements

Aspects of Chapters 1 and 4 of this book were published as articles in the *LSE Public Policy Review* (in articles titled "A Little Give and Take" and "An Unhappy Pursuit of Happiness"), of Chapter 6 in *Behavioural Public Policy* (in an article titled "Sir John Stuffgut's Soup and a Taste for Desert") and of Chapters 7 and 8 in the *Journal of European Public Policy* (in an article titled "Reviving and Revising Economic Liberalism: An Examination in Relation to Private Decisions and Public Policy" [Oliver, 2020]).

I owe thanks to a number of people in the writing of my trilogy on behavioural public policy. I have acknowledged them in the two previous books. For this book I will limit my thanks to Phil Good at Cambridge University Press and to the three reviewers that he solicited to provide detailed comments on a previous version of the entire manuscript; to Keti and Charlie, who, as ever, offer benefits without substantive harms; and to David Hume and, particularly, John Stuart Mill, who, although somewhat taxing at times, have been, on the whole, good company.

Introduction

As noted in the Preface, this book forms the final part of my trilogy on behavioural public policy. The first book in the series, *The Origins of Behavioural Public Policy* (a title inspired by Charles Darwin's *On the Origin of Species*) was followed by *Reciprocity and the Art of Behavioural Public Policy* (a title inspired by Robert Pirsig's *Zen and the Art of Motorcycle Maintenance*). The title of the current volume, as also mentioned in the Preface, was inspired by Mill's *Principles of Political Economy*.[1] By way of introduction, before proceeding to the main body of the current text, it is therefore apt, I think, to detail briefly where, in my discussions of behavioural public policy, I have so far been, and where I intend to go.

WHERE I HAVE BEEN

My aim in the *Origins* book was to outline the foundations and development of the relatively new subfield of behavioural public policy.[2] Given that behavioural public policy is defined as the use of behavioural economics, and behavioural science more broadly, to inform public policy design, that book necessarily included a brief summary of the development of behavioural economics, and indeed of standard rational choice theory also.[3] In that vein, broadly speaking, the book considered two principal lines of inquiry: namely, the early challenges that questioned the descriptive validity of the axioms of expected utility theory (e.g. the Allais and Ellsberg paradoxes), and the suggestion that people employ decision-making heuristics – which challenges the assumption that they maximise expected utility – and which is associated heavily with Herbert Simon and, later, Daniel Kahneman and Amos Tversky.

The behavioural phenomena – present bias, loss aversion, anchoring, reciprocal motivations, etc. – that had been written about intuitively hundreds of years ago by writers such as Adam Smith (1759/2009), were validated empirically by modern behavioural economists and psychologists in those lines of inquiry, and it is these phenomena that form the building blocks of behavioural public policy. In the *Origins* book, I discussed many of the questions that these behavioural scientists had posed for standard economic and rational choice theory assumptions pertaining to time, to utility, and to money, while at the same recognising – indeed, advocating – that the foundations of behavioural public policy are built not just from contributions by economists and psychologists, but from all of the other social sciences, from the humanities, and from branches of the natural sciences (e.g. biology and zoology) also.

I also reviewed some of the principal conceptual behavioural public policy frameworks that had, at that point, been developed, and highlighted that hard and, particularly, soft forms of paternalism had dominated – and still dominate – behavioural public policy (at least in terms of the rhetoric if not actual policy applications).[4] This paternalistic focus is, I believe, a mistake, for reasons that I will consider in some depth in this third book of the trilogy.[5] At the end of the *Origins* book I chose to highlight how reciprocity, in contrast to the selfish egoism that is typically cited as a characteristic of rational choice, is perhaps the most powerful human motivational force, as recognised by its prominent place in the discourses within a range of disciplines. Yet it seemed to me that the consideration of how to use reciprocal motivations as an input to design better public policies had been strangely lacking.

The discourse on human motivation with respect to policy design has instead tended to focus on the dichotomy between selfish egoism and pure altruism. I argued in the *Origins* book that encouraging selfish egoism, even if done so with the intention of improving public sector performance, may well damage the ethos on which the provision of good public services is based, and relying on pure altruism, which is a relatively rare form of human motivation, is naïve. Reciprocity assumes that we give and take, rather than unconditionally give or take, and serves to strengthen cooperative activities within groups. Therefore, it is important for any group-based dynamic that this tendency is not crowded out by policy interventions that assume that people are predominantly egoistical.

I will not be revealing any secrets by stating that the principal focus in the second book in my trilogy was reciprocity. The intention in that second book was to continue and greatly expand upon the themes that I introduced briefly at the end of the first book. The main objectives of the second book were to review reciprocity from a number of different disciplinary perspectives, and to explore in more depth how policy design might be informed by that motivational force. I began the book by contending that reciprocity lies deep within the human psyche (and in a basic form, is observed in the behaviours of many non-human species also), with there being evidence that very small children show tendencies towards both positive and negative reciprocity.[6]

I argued that the fundamental reason why people (and some other animals) act reciprocally is to bring forth benefits and protection to the group, and, by extension, to the individual members of the group. Thus, social norms of both positive and negative reciprocity evolved from a form of self-interest – albeit a more long-term form of self-interest than that associated with selfish egoism, the latter of which may serve some people very well in the short term, but which can erode group cohesion and ultimately be of detriment to one's longer-term objectives. Labelling positive reciprocity as reciprocal altruism is common, but is therefore something of a misnomer, because it is unlikely that a purely altruistic urge underpins this motivational force.

In the *Reciprocity* book I also noted that a further way to discern how deep within our species this or any other motivational force lies – in addition to studying the behaviours of human children and non-human animals – is to attempt to glean some understanding of how our ancestors lived, which can by proxy be done by observing extant tribal communities. It has widely been reported that both positive and negative reciprocity, in relation to, for example, the sharing of meat, childcare responsibilities and wisdom, and as a means of building obligations and discouraging power grabs, are crucial to the proper functioning of those communities.

In addition to touching upon evolutionary psychology, animal behaviouralism and anthropology, I referred to some of the work that behavioural economists, often in collaboration with psychologists, have undertaken on reciprocity, principally using economic games under controlled laboratory conditions. If one leans heavily on reciprocal motivations in building a conceptual framework for behavioural public policy, it is obviously important to consider the now quite extensive body of work that behavioural economists – principally, Ernst Fehr and his colleagues – have undertaken on the topic. These experiments demonstrate that the extent to which reciprocity is observed and sustained is likely to be dependent on context, with repetition of the game, the inclusion or not of punishment, anonymity between partners, whether the money on offer is windfall or earned, and many other factors having an influence. Therefore, although the tendency to act reciprocally appears to be almost hardwired within us, the context – the environment – that people face can crowd in or crowd out this motivational force. Thus, the two-word essence of behavioural public policy is evident – i.e. context matters – and thus an environment conducive to the reciprocal instincts needs to be in place if they are to produce their full benefit.

It ought to be admitted – and it was indeed emphasised in the second book – that there are also some devilish aspects of reciprocity, including, but not limited to, its potential to strengthen mutually reinforcing subgroups who discriminate against perceived outsiders, its capacity to generate power imbalances by imposing unwanted obligations and, with respect to negative reciprocity, the possibility of instituting seemingly endless spirals of retaliation. The increased polarisation in the political discourse in several countries over recent

years, with social media and a heightened readiness by certain politicians and their followers to stoke widespread paranoia playing an
interrelated disharmonising role, demonstrates that reciprocity and
cooperation within particular groupings poses an ever-present threat
to the social fabric of society as a whole. But if harnessed carefully so
that it helps to create and sustain opportunities for all people to
flourish, reciprocity can serve substantively as a beneficial force. In
the *Reciprocity* book, I discussed some ways in which the policy-
making environment, and society in general, might be designed in
order to realise the benefits of our reciprocal instincts. These
included an emphasis on public policy decentralisation, because
securing reciprocal motivations and abating egoistical ones is easier
in relatively smaller groups, and the reversal of the income and
wealth concentrations in very small percentages of populations that
have become much more pronounced in many countries over the last
four decades, because they erode social cohesion and may legitimise
unconditional "taking".

At the end of the book, I briefly introduced a new political
economy of behavioural public policy informed substantively by reciprocity, one that eschewed the paternalism that is central to the
dominant forms of behavioural public policy to date. I argued that
affording people a great deal of individual autonomy within some very
broad environmental parameters (e.g. localised decision-making, reasonably equitable income and wealth distributions) is an effective way
by which to secure social cooperation, and will help people to flourish
in both achieving the objectives of their public sector services, and in
them realising their multifarious privately held desires in life. That
said, I recognised that affording people a great deal of individual
autonomy will likely result in those who are egoistically inclined
to attempt to exploit others by using, implicitly or explicitly,
behavioural-informed tactics. Therefore, in addition to offering a great
deal of autonomy as a means of nurturing reciprocity among those
who impose no substantive harms on others, I suggested that an
overarching conceptual framework of behavioural public policy must

also include a second arm, one that calls for regulations against behavioural-informed harms to others – i.e. the threat of a form of negative reciprocity. The framework that I suggested fits within the liberal tradition, particularly that postulated by Wilhelm von Humboldt (1791–1792/1993) and John Stuart Mill (1859/1969).[7] The principal objective of this, the final part of the trilogy, is to further develop my preferred overarching political economy of behavioural public policy.

WHERE I AM GOING

As already stated, the objective of the book you have before you is to build an overarching conceptual framework – a political economy – of behavioural public policy that gives guidance on where applications of this relatively new subfield of public policy are legitimate. This is the first all-enveloping policy framework in this policy domain and is a framework that is offered in the spirit of the liberal tradition.[8] First, however, I offer a disclaimer, with reference to the circumstances that we are living through at the time of writing. This is not a book about the Covid-19 pandemic or climate change or any other (relatively fleeting or more sustained) policy challenge. I do refer to these and other policy challenges throughout the book by way of illustrating the various arguments, but to have focused on, for example, the Covid-19 pandemic would have given the book a more limited shelf life, and ultimately a narrower influence, than I hope for.[9] Rather, the book provides a framework within which the legitimacy of any policy challenge that is, at least in part, addressable with behavioural public policy interventions can be considered; and that probably encompasses all conceivable policy challenges.

Typically, the paternalistic vision for behavioural public policy is that people, due to the behavioural phenomena that can influence their choices, make mistakes. That is to say, people often choose, decide and behave in violation of that which maximises their lifetime welfare (or utility), that they are thus being irrational, and that there is therefore a justification for manipulating, or even coercing, them for their own good. However, if the behavioural phenomena that are frequently labelled as "biases" are so ingrained in the human psyche, then presumably they must have evolved for good reasons, and therefore, strictly speaking, they may not be biasing influences at all. It may be the case that other parties take advantage of their implicit or explicit knowledge of these influences in order to manipulate people into doing things that they would rather not do, but in the absence of such manipulation, and given that people may have multifarious objectives in their own personal lives (with many of those objectives having little to do with welfare or utility maximisation), can a third party really conclude that their actions and behaviours are mistaken? A challenge to the assumption that the behavioural phenomena are necessarily biasing influences, and thus an implicit challenge to the legitimacy of paternalistic behavioural public policy, is laid out in Chapter 1.

In Chapter 2, however, I feel that it is only fair to summarise the parameters of some of the existing (albeit narrower) behavioural public policy frameworks, partly so that readers can reach their own conclusions with respect to the legitimacy of each framework and partly to serve as a reference against which my proposed political economy can be contrasted and compared. In Chapter 3, I note that several scholars have expressed support for soft forms of paternalism by arguing that humans are limited in their reasoning abilities: namely, that they (or rather, we) are limited in imagination, willpower, objectivity and technical skills. These scholars argue that, as a consequence, individuals sometimes fail in their pursuit of that for which they ought to be striving – specifically, more welfare, utility or happiness. Therefore, they need the guiding hand of the policy maker.

Countering these claims, in Chapter 4 I question whether utility (or welfare or happiness) maximisation is a legitimate general normative goal of public policy by arguing that, often, the pursuit of utility does not drive desires. Rather, desires typically precede any consideration of utility. Desires, I contend, are multifarious and vary across people and, with a nod to Chapter 1, may be meaningfully facilitated by the behavioural influences. Thus, I contend that over the private realm of individual decision-making, the policy maker's role should not equate with being a utility-maximising social planner; rather, a policy maker should seek to secure the general conditions that facilitate people in their pursuit of their own conception of the desired life. Building on the arguments I initiated in the *Reciprocity* book, I contend in Chapter 5 that this can best be achieved by allowing people a great deal of autonomy. Liberals (such as myself) maintain that autonomous actions are the most effective way of forging the social cooperation from which we all benefit.

In Chapter 6, I suggest that reciprocity is linked heavily to perceptions of desert, which itself underpins notions of justice. This again therefore may underline how a motivational force that arose organically to benefit the individual by protecting the group to which he belonged evolved into a normative concept.[10] I argue that desert-based reciprocity is informed by considerations both of intentions and outcomes, which is useful when thinking about how public support for public sector services and broader welfare systems might be maintained. In Chapters 7 and 8 I continue the theme of how one might use reciprocity to inform policy design, first over the domain of private individual decision-making and then over the domain of public sector decision-making. For the former, due to the differing and multifarious desires that people may have (including the desire to start one's own business and the desire to escape from a poor-quality service), I conclude that disallowing the competitive market would be too much of an infringement on individual liberty, but for the latter, where public sector services exist to deliver a limited range of a priori collectively agreed-upon goals, the risks associated with market failures and the exploitation of the behavioural influences ought to cause us to be more circumspect of the potential net benefit of demand-led competition. In these circumstances, it is argued, and from the perspective of my political economy of behavioural public policy, reputational competition is more legitimate.

In Chapter 9, I elaborate on how policy might be used to regulate against those who, through self-serving actions, abuse their autonomy by imposing behaviourally informed harms on others. Typically, these actions will distort the mechanism of a fair exchange and will thus undermine the very notion of a reciprocal relationship, but sometimes they involve inaction rather than action, when action could deliver easily won benefits. This arm of my political economy of behavioural public policy includes regulations against both negative externalities and regulations to produce positive externalities; in short, it proposes that in order to protect freedom in general, some specific freedoms will need to be curtailed.

Thus, as aforementioned, this book explicates the political economy of behavioural public policy that I initially mooted in the *Reciprocity* book, but the short synopsis of that framework remains the same. That is, that policy makers ought to nurture the reciprocal instincts that evolved among humans for group and individual benefit by influencing the very general conditions of society that facilitate that objective, while at the same time regulating those who harm others by using the behavioural influences to exploit the opportunities that have been granted them. I hope I have not given too much away in this short introduction to dissuade the reader from reading on, but that I have given away enough to entice the reader to read on, and, indeed, to read "back", if they have not yet read the first two books in the trilogy.

I   Setting the Scene

In his introduction to the Pelican Classics edition of John Stuart Mill's *Principles of Political Economy*, the economist Donald Winch wrote that:

> Like all liberal theorists, [Mill] took the individual as the basic unit of discourse. His contact with traditions antagonistic to the one in which he was brought up merely served to strengthen his attachment to individualism by enlarging his conception of what individuality should comprise. Institutional arrangements in society should be judged basically in terms of whether they enhanced this individuality by widening the sphere of independence and choice. In so far as social, political and economic conditions inhibited or prevented individuals, or groups of individuals such as the working classes, from partaking fully in the benefits of the social union, these should be removed by direct intervention or negative prohibition.
>
> *(Winch, 1970, p.48)*

In essence, Mill, according to Winch, believed that in order to protect liberty in general, some specific freedoms ought to be constrained, a view that had also been held by John Locke. From a behavioural public policy perspective, this will also be my conclusion in this book.

However, before reaching my conclusion it may prove instructive to detail how I arrived at it. As noted in the Introduction, in a previous book I contended that the motivational force of reciprocity – of responding in kind to good, and bad, intentions and/or actions – can and should be nurtured by policy makers to aid individuals in the pursuit of their own private predilections and public sector groupings in the pursuit of their collective objectives (Oliver, 2019). To borrow from the economist Amartya Sen (1999), to the extent that public sector services, such as health and education, provide people with the capabilities to pursue their privately held goals in life, an environment that crowds in reciprocal motivations in those sectors is perfectly consistent with sustaining and extending liberty. As I previously contended, the urge to act reciprocally – and a concern with that which facilitates indirect reciprocity (namely, a good reputation) – lies deep within the human psyche, and probably evolved because this motivational force brings forth benefits and protection to the group.[1] Moreover, and importantly, since the individuals that comprise a group are more likely to fare well if their group is flourishing, a reciprocal cooperative spirit is compatible with – indeed, is probably principally driven by – the pursuit of individual long-term self-interest. Hence, out of this evolutionary process arose instinctive tendencies and social norms that favour conditional cooperation and that justify punishment of those who transgress.

Admittedly, that subgroups often act cooperatively and reciprocally to the detriment of the wider group is an unfortunate possibility that has long been recognised. The Scottish Enlightenment philosopher David Hume, for instance, wrote that 'Factions subvert government, render laws impotent, and beget the fiercest animosities among men of the same nation, who ought to give mutual assistance and protection to each other' (Hume, 1777/2018, p.155). Hume elsewhere noted that 'Robbers and pirates ... could not maintain their pernicious confederacy, did they not establish a new distributive justice among themselves, and recall those laws of equity, which they have violated with the rest of mankind' (Hume, 1751/2018, pp.33–34). There are also risks associated with negative reciprocity, including undue or excessive retribution and spiralling retaliation, but if harnessed in the right way reciprocity can serve substantively as a force for good, as also emphasised by Hume, as we shall later see.

Reciprocity as a motivational force can, and sometimes is, embraced, if peripherally, by several different behavioural public policy frameworks, but is central to that favoured in this book;

namely, to nurture reciprocity in the positive sense so that people may be able to better pursue their own conception of a flourishing life, and also in the negative sense, to constrain those who might otherwise exploit the liberty that has been granted to them and in doing so impose unacceptable harms on others.[2] Given the centrality of reciprocity to this framework, it seems apt at this point to reflect a little further on the concept.[3]

THE ORIGIN OF RECIPROCITY

Those who write on the evolutionary origin of reciprocity present varied, if related, arguments. The evolutionary biologist Joseph Henrich, for instance, sees reciprocity as underpinning the mutual protection that became ever more necessary after our ancestors descended the trees and became ground apes (Henrich, 2016), whereas the ethologist and primatologist Christopher Boehm notes that reciprocal tendencies strengthen as a necessary feature of insurance when individual success in a hunt is uncertain (Boehm, 2012).[4] Boehm reports that when chimpanzees hunt, those that gain initial control of the carcass will share just enough to enable them to retain control, and there may be reciprocation between givers and receivers when their relative success (or lack thereof) is reversed in the future.[5] According to Boehm, archaic homo sapiens killed larger game than do chimpanzees, and thus there was more sharing, and in hunter-gatherer societies dominance over meat was often negated entirely by having it shared out by a neutral person (see also Sapolsky, 2017, p.323).

In *Utilitarianism*, Mill (1863/1969) wrote that we control ourselves in the face of internal and external sanctions, with the internal mediated by our conscience, but that our feelings for others, where they exist at all, are much weaker than our feelings for ourselves. Mill further contended that where feelings for others exist they do so due to a concern for their utility – a concern for *them*. One might acknowledge Mill's view, but it seems that a concern for others evolved because that is the best means to serve oneself, at least in the long term. Despite the different nuances of the evolutionary arguments presented in the previous paragraph, these explanations share a common underlying reason for the origin of reciprocity; namely, that reciprocation and cooperation arose not from altruism in the pure sense of the term (i.e. from unconditional giving), but from a sense of individual self-interest.[6] This is not self-interest in the form of avaricious egoism (i.e. a desire to benefit oneself irrespective of the consequences for others), but rather an implicit recognition – an evolved sense – that whatever benefits the groups in which we find ourselves is likely to benefit us also.

Presumably, few would doubt that humans are influenced by a mix of motives, including those that can be characterised as reciprocal, egoistic and perhaps even altruistic, or that the relative strengths of these motivations vary both interpersonally and, over time and context, intrapersonally. Hume acknowledged this long ago when he wrote that 'there is some benevolence, however, small, infused into our bosom; some spark of friendship for human kind; some particle of the dove kneaded into our frame, along with the elements of the wolf and the serpent' (Hume, 1751/2018, p.78). However, the view that people are often driven to benefit others ultimately to benefit themselves has a long history in political philosophy. For example, in the middle of the nineteenth century, the political scientist Alexis de Tocqueville, in his seminal *Democracy in America*, wrote that 'The Americans ... are fond of explaining almost all the actions of their lives by the principle of self-interest rightly understood; they show with complacency how an enlightened regard for themselves constantly prompts them to assist one another and inclines them willingly to sacrifice a portion of their time and property to the welfare of the state' (de Tocqueville, 1835/1998, p.230).[7]

Earlier still, Hume himself suggested that cooperation and reciprocity evolved organically over eons when the mutuality that is necessary for small family units to subsist eventually extends to cover whole societies; he wrote, suppose the conjunction of the sexes to be established in nature, a family immediately arises and particular rules being found requisite for its subsistence, these are immediately embraced; though without comprehending the rest of mankind within their prescriptions. Suppose that several families unite together into one society, which is totally disjoined from all others, the rules, which preserve peace and order, enlarge themselves to the utmost extent of that society; but becoming then entirely useless, lose their force when carried one step further. But again suppose, that several distinct societies maintain a kind of intercourse for mutual convenience and advantage, the boundaries of justice still grow larger, in proportion to the largeness of men's views, and the force of their mutual connexions. History, experience, reason sufficiently instruct us in this natural progress of human sentiments, and in the gradual enlargement of our regards to justice, in proportion as we become acquainted with the extensive utility of that virtue.

(Hume, 1751/2018, p.20)[8]

He went on to infer, a little more succinctly, that reciprocity evolved because it benefits each party to an exchange; that

two men pull the oars of a boat by common convention for common interest, without any promise or contract . . .. Whatever is advantageous to two or more persons, if all perform their part; but what loses all advantage if only one perform, can arise from no other principle. There would otherwise be no motive for any one of them to enter into that scheme of conduct.

(Hume, 1751/2018, p.103)

Assuming that reciprocity is a fundamental motivator of human behaviour does not negate the possibility that the other motivations, particularly the more selfishly egoistic driver, can in some circumstances crowd out the notion of give and take for one of take and take some more, which could ultimately be detrimental to the group and the individuals of whom it is comprised. Thus, we might conclude that in hunter-gatherer societies (and perhaps before), reciprocity evolved for the good of the group and its individual members, but that as societies grew and became more atomised, opportunities were in turn furthered for the egoistically inclined to act upon their motivations with less fear of being observed. Thus, a form of social contract, manifested in most of the world's major religious codes and embedded in laws, became necessary to reinforce the socially beneficial norm of (positive and negative) reciprocity. Hume acknowledged the strengthening effect of laws on civility, believing that even in his day the modern administration of government had attained a very advanced state of 'humanity, clemency, order, tranquillity, and the other social virtues' that, he claimed, would have amazed the ancient Greeks (Hume, 1751/2018 , p.68).

Since the focus of this book is to offer a new political economy of behavioural public policy, I will at this point offer some thoughts on how particular evolutionary explanations of the two forms of self-interest considered – i.e. egoistic and enlightened self-interest – might relate to perhaps the most important implication of prospect theory, inarguably the most influential behavioural economic theory that has thus far been developed. The influence of prospect theory includes it having had a prominent role in the development of behavioural public policy, and it is typically held by behavioural economists that this theory predicts that humans are systematically biased in their decision-making. However, these predicted behaviours, which are sometimes observed, may be deemed perfectly reasonable when considered in the contexts in which they likely evolved.

SCARCITY, ABUNDANCE AND REFLECTION

In times of extreme scarcity and shortages, it may be rational to be an egoist.[9] Indeed, your very survival could depend on it. In his study of the Netsilik Inuit people of Northern Canada, Boehm (2012, p.219) acknowledges as such when he writes that the 'capacity to make strategic decisions ... enabled people like the hungry Netsilik to reject their own customary sharing practices when food became so scarce that trusting in a long-term system of indirect reciprocity became life threatening. At that point, the group social control that kept such systems going would simply fade away.' With food that scarce, one can either choose between being an egoist and face a chance of starving, or being a reciprocator and definitely starve. Commenting on native Americans a little further south, de Tocqueville contended that they were often forced into egoism due to scarcity induced by the encroachment of Europeans:

> The Indians, who had previously lived in a sort of abundance, then find it difficult to subsist, and still more difficult to procure the articles of barter that they stand in need of . . .. At length they are compelled to . . . depart . . .. It is impossible to conceive the frightful sufferings that attend these forced migrations . . .. Hunger is in the rear, war awaits them, and misery besets them on all sides. To escape from so many enemies, they separate, and each individual endeavours to procure secretly the means of supporting his existence by isolating himself, living in the immensity of the desert like an outcast in civilised society. The social tie, which distress had long since weakened, is then dissolved.
>
> *(de Tocqueville, 1835/1998, p.137–138)*[10]

Thus, when want is widespread, people are perhaps driven by necessity to behave in ways that mirror individual selection; that is, they are fully focused on their own survival in the moment. On the flip side, if everything that is desired is so abundant that most people could easily satisfy the majority of their desires via their own efforts, perhaps egoism would also dominate, because there would be little need to cooperate and reciprocate. However, it is probably reasonable to assume that most people, the majority of the time, face neither extreme scarcity nor enjoy unlimited abundance in either hunter-gatherer or modern societies. It is somewhere between these extremes, where cooperation may best serve people's interests, that is the more common circumstance.

To see how these contextual motivations might relate to modern behavioural economic theory, let us turn, as promised, to prospect theory – developed by the psychologists Daniel Kahneman and Amos Tversky (Kahneman and Tversky, 1979; Tversky and Kahneman, 1992). Prospect theory essentially makes two principal modifications to the standard theory of rational choice (i.e. von Neumann–Morgenstern expected utility theory): first, rather than final assets, the subjective carriers of value are assumed to be gains and losses around a "reference point" – with the reference point generally assumed to be the status quo, the accustomed position, the most likely or expected outcome, or the aspiration level – and with losses weighted roughly twice as much as gains of the same magnitude (which implies loss aversion); and second, it is assumed that probabilities are subjectively weighted, such that low probabilities are overweighted and high probabilities are underweighted, rather than processed in their objective mathematical form. Tversky and Kahneman (1992, p.306) state that the 'most distinctive implication of prospect theory is the fourfold pattern of risk attitudes' known as the reflection effect. Note the significance of this effect as the most distinctive implication of the most influential alternative to the dominant economic theory of rational choice. The fourfold pattern of risk attitudes is summarised in Table 1.1.

The top left quadrant in Table 1.1 summarises the prospect theory risk attitude prediction when a person is faced with a large probability of a gain – for example, a 0.99 chance of winning £1,000 and a 0.01 chance of winning nothing. If an individual is offered a choice between this risky option and the certainty of its expected value of £990 (i.e. 0.99*1,000), prospect theory predicts that the

Table 1.1 *The reflection effect*

	Gains	Losses
High Probability **(The Certainty Effect)**	Fear of Missing Gain Risk Aversion	Hope to Avoid Loss Risk Seeking
Low Probability **(The Possibility Effect)**	Hope of Gain Risk Seeking	Fear of Loss Risk Aversion

individual will place a high weight on the certainty, will reject the risky option and will thus display risk aversion.[11] The bottom left quadrant summarises the predicted risk attitude when a person is faced with a small probability of a gain, such as a 0.01 chance of winning £1,000 and a 0.99 chance of winning nothing. Here, prospect theory predicts that the individual will overweight the chance of winning, would thus prefer the gamble over its expected value of £10 (i.e. 0.01 * 1,000), and will therefore be risk seeking. The top and bottom right quadrants of Table 1.1 can be read similarly, and show that prospect theory predicts opposing risk attitudes for losses as compared to gains in both large and small probability scenarios.[12] That the predicted risk attitudes are apparently reflected across gains and losses for both high and low probabilities gives the reflection effect its name; this fourfold pattern of risk attitudes contrasts with that of universal mild risk aversion or risk neutrality predicted by standard rational choice theory.

Tversky and Kahneman (1992) provided some empirical support for the full fourfold pattern of risk attitudes, but perhaps strangely given the import of the reflection effect to modern behavioural economic theory, controlled testing of the full effect is quite scarce. Moreover, the evidence that has been gathered is somewhat mixed, with support seemingly to some extent dependent on the magnitude of the outcomes used (see Oliver, 2018, and the references therein). There are several possible explanations for why this evidence is mixed. For example, perhaps the methods used by researchers are not always entirely fit for purpose, or it could be the case that the data is not always analysed appropriately. Or perhaps prospect theory, like the standard theory of rational choice, in assuming that people will assess a risky option by somewhat mechanistically weighting the subjective value of its outcomes with their associated (weighted or unweighted) probabilities, does not fully describe the processes that have evolved to help humans deal with uncertainty.

Anatomically modern humans emerged 200,000 years ago and hunter-gathering was the dominant form of social organisation until the development of agriculture about 12,000 years ago. The consideration of well-defined probabilities, used in games of chance, stretches back only a few centuries, although through the avenues of formal education and pastimes such as gambling on sporting outcomes, a widespread exposure to well-defined probabilities is more recent than that.[13] It is thus plausible that the way in which humans deal with uncertain events now is still influenced heavily by the processes that evolved to help our hunter-gatherer ancestors (and their predecessors) deal with uncertainty in their search for food (and sexual partners), which are likely to have been driven by perceptions of frequency of success, based on recent experience, and by magnitude of outcome.

If food was considered to be relatively abundant due to high rates of recent success and sizable prey, it is likely that hunters would be less inclined to take risks to secure food than if it was relatively scarce simply because they did not need to in order to satisfy their immediate needs.[14] Their focus may well have been on securing sufficient food to sustain themselves over the relative short term, rather than the maximisation of expected value.[15] If the likelihood of securing a good catch was high but still involved an element of risk, such a pursuit would implicitly have a high expected value; however, there would still be a chance of failure, which could have catastrophic consequences. An alternative strategy that promised a less impressive but still sufficient catch but with less or no risk attached to it may well have had a lower expected value (in terms of calorific content, perhaps), but if it had a higher chance of sustaining life by guaranteeing sustenance, it would be a sensible strategy to pursue, particularly in the absence of any facility for the long-term storage of meat.[16]

Conversely, if food was thought to be scarce due to infrequent recent hunting successes and modest prey, then without taking risks people may have realised that there would be an insufficient catch to sustain them. In this circumstance, the expected value of a risky hunting expedition would equate to a very modest, possibly worthless, catch. Although the hunters would not have calculated the expected value of the hunt with any degree of accuracy, they would have had to have been guaranteed a haul very much greater than the expected value in order to feel that the guarantee is sufficient to offset the risk. Implicitly, through necessity, they would have been driven to seek risk.

The two scenarios just described – i.e. high and low frequencies of success, signalling relative abundance and scarcity – respectively mirror the top and bottom left quadrants of Table 1.1, where probability serves as a proxy for prior frequency of success. With decent sized (but not enormous) gains a possibility, there seems to be reasonable evolutionary – natural selection – explanations for why people may implicitly display the risk attitudes predicted by prospect theory.[17] But what about the right-hand quadrants that focus on potential losses?

Let us first consider the top right-hand quadrant – a high probability of a loss, implying, in an evolutionary sense, a high frequency of recent losses, in turn implying relative scarcity. It seems unlikely that our hunter-gatherer ancestors would have ventured out on a hunt when the best possible outcome was to catch nothing at all, and thus we can assume that it may seem quite unnatural for people to consider a gamble that offers only a chance of an absolute loss and a corresponding chance of nothing. In such circumstances, the reference point that people adopt might be their aspiration level rather than the status quo, and indeed hunter-gatherers may have viewed any game caught that did not reach something a little above their subsistence requirements (i.e. their minimum aspiration level of a comfortable amount of food) not as a gain, but as a loss. If potential losses in this scenario are interpreted as such, one may take the view that the only thing that can offer salvation is the small chance of meeting subsistence requirements – or, at any rate, that a guaranteed loss that is anything close to the expected loss of the gamble is unhelpful for survival. If this reasoning is correct, then the analogue of a high probability loss is not a high probability gain, as is generally assumed under prospect theory; rather, it is a low probability gain, and a similar attitude of risk seeking, inconsistent with the predictions of standard rational choice theory, is expected.

This just leaves the low probability of a loss in the bottom right-hand quadrant, which if one's aspiration level is again the reference point, might imply relative abundance. That is, there is only a small chance that the hunter-gatherer will not secure his aspiration of a comfortable amount of food; but there is a chance nonetheless, and if it does come to pass it could spell disaster. In such a situation one may be willing to sacrifice an amount that is somewhat higher than the small expected loss of the risky option in order to guarantee the avoidance of catastrophe (but the sacrifice would still be small, and thus one would be trading off only a small proportion of one's aspiration level, which is manageable).[18] In effect, we would see implied risk aversion in this standard insurance scenario, a situation that parallels, with a consistent risk attitude, the high probability gain in the top left quadrant. Here, the analogue of the low probability loss is therefore not a low probability gain; it is a high probability gain, with expected implied risk aversion that is consistent with the predictions of both standard rational choice theory and prospect theory.

If the above interpretations are correct, then when potential outcomes are decent but not enormous, people will out of necessity act in a way that implies greater risk seeking in circumstances of relative scarcity than those of relative abundance. When food was relatively abundant (or at least not extremely scarce) but not guaranteed, people may have evolved strategies where they were willing to give up some of their catch when they were fortunate in the expectation that those they shared with would reciprocate when their fortunes were reversed, which is, as alluded to in endnote 16, in essence a risk-averse insurance strategy that ensures stable sustenance (and is essentially Boehm's (2012) explanation for the origin of reciprocity mentioned earlier). When food was very scarce with a low frequency of a successful catch, on the other hand, then unless the catch is very large, people might not be in a position to share any of it; they may need the entire catch just to survive, and thus they may be forced to continue to take risks, to be egoistic and hope to survive until a period of relative abundance returns.[19]

To sum up, when resources are limited, as they invariably are, but we are not in desperate need, we tend to share in order to increase our individual security. This cooperation – these reciprocal actions – mitigate the misfortune that we might experience if we relied entirely on ourselves. Negative reciprocity – the threat and act of punishment – at least in part emerged to crowd in expected positive reciprocity among those who might otherwise transgress, and thus inevitably places constraints on the freedoms of those who are egoistically inclined. In short and to reiterate from the Introduction to this book, to protect freedom and security in general, some specific freedoms must be constrained.

CONSTRAINING FREEDOM

As aforementioned, it is my contention in this book that in most circumstances an evolved sense of long-term self-interest is good for most – perhaps all – people in a society. The political economy of behavioural public policy that I will propose calls for a nurturing of these reciprocal instincts, which, if undertaken with care, may help people in the pursuit of their privately held goals in life, whatever those goals might be, and may facilitate the public sector in meeting its predetermined broadly agreed-upon objectives. Thus, the argument will be that the general environment and our institutions and policies should be shaped so as to crowd in the beneficial effects of reciprocity. So long as the general structures of society are conducive to cooperative behaviours, there is, I maintain, no call for policies that interfere too much in the choices that people make, so long as those choices are not harming others; if you allow people to be free, most have the (evolved) mental apparatus to seek and find practices of mutual benefit without the hands-on involvement of third parties who claim to know better.[20]

That said, great freedom, without any counteracting measures, does of course offer a lot of scope for the egoistically inclined to act upon their motives, and can indeed serve those people very well, certainly in the short term, but also in the long term if their behaviours go undetected and/or unpunished and do not fundamentally damage the groups to which they belong. Hume believed that being seduced as such was more often caused by weakness than by malicious intentions. He commented that:

> Some extraordinary circumstances may happen, in which a man finds his interests to be more promoted by fraud or rapine, than hurt by the breach which his injustice makes in the social union. But much more frequently, he is seduced from his great and important, but distant interests, by the allurement of present, though often very frivolous temptations. This great weakness is incurable in human nature.
>
> *(Hume, 1777/2018, p.151)*

Whether fraudulent or frivolous (or both, or neither), egoistic actions have the potential to harm the wider group.[21] Consequently, Hume, like his friend Adam Smith, saw the threat of negative reciprocity as vital in sustaining justice and in holding society together, maintaining that '[m]en must ... institute some persons ... whose peculiar office it is ... to punish transgressors, to correct fraud and violence, and to oblige men, however reluctant, to consult their own real and permanent interests' (Hume, 1777/2018, p. 151). Hume ultimately felt that despite our inclination to act reciprocally, there could be no civilised society without laws, magistrates and judges, serving to discourage egoists from manipulating, coercing, exploiting or otherwise harming others.[22]

Ludwig von Mises, a doyen of the Austrian School of Economics, a group of thinkers who are associated with free market liberalism, also saw the threat of negative reciprocity as foundational to the proper functioning of society. 'The liberal understands quite clearly', he wrote,

> that without resort to compulsion, the existence of society would be endangered and that behind the rules of conduct whose observance is necessary to assure peaceful human cooperation must

stand the threat of force if the whole edifice of society is not to be
continually at the mercy of any one of its members. One must be in
a position to compel the person who will not respect the lives,
health, personal freedom, or private property of others to acquiesce
in the rules of life in society. This is the function that the liberal
doctrine assigns the state: the protection of property, liberty,
and peace.

(von Mises, 1927/2005, p.17)

On this, von Mises is close to Mill's famous harm principle,
which states

[t]hat the only purpose for which power can be rightfully exercised
over any member of a civilised community, against his will, is to
prevent harm to others. His own good, either physical or moral, is
not a sufficient warrant. He cannot rightfully be compelled to do or
forbear because it will be better for him to do so, because it will
make him happier, because, in the opinions of others, to do so
would be wise, or even right. These are good reasons for
remonstrating with him, or reasoning with him, or persuading him,
or entreating him, but not for compelling him, or visiting him with
any evil in case he do otherwise.

(Mill, 1859/1969, pp.12–13)[23]

The contention in this book is that nor are these good reasons for
manipulating him. In his introduction to Mill's book, the philosopher
Isaiah Berlin wrote that '[m]en want to curtail the liberties of other
men, either *(a)* because they wish to impose their power on others; or
(b) because they want conformity ... or, finally, *(c)* because they
believe that to the question of how one should live there can be ...
one true answer and one only' (Berlin, 1969, p.xviii). From a behavioural public policy perspective, I will argue that there is a further
reason for curtailing liberties: that is, to prevent those who might
(often implicitly) use the instruments of behavioural science (for
example, the phenomena embedded within, and the implications of,
prospect theory, that I have argued are consistent with behaviours

that may have evolved for good reasons in other circumstances), typically by distorting the exchange relationship, to benefit themselves and impose unreasonable harms on others.[24]

Thus, in sum (and, for emphasis, to once again repeat from the Introduction), the political economy of behavioural public policy that I will propose as the most appropriate way forward for this still relatively new field of analysis is one that respects freedom over actions that do not negatively affect others, but that nurtures reciprocity, both in its positive form in order to better equip people in the pursuit of privately held and policy-related objectives, and in its negative form in justifying regulation against behavioural-informed harms. It is, I argue, an approach that sits firmly within the liberal tradition. Of course, not everyone will agree with my direction of travel, and thus before developing my arguments further, it is I think necessary to at least acknowledge some of the other possible routes.

FOOD FOR THOUGHT

1. Do we reciprocate mostly to benefit others or ourselves?
2. When might it be necessary to be an egoist, and when might it be sensible not to be?
3. Is negative reciprocity essential to the proper functioning of society?

2   Other Voices

It will I hope by now be clear to the reader that my preferred political economy of behavioural public policy attaches great weight to the importance of individual autonomy unless people are imposing externalities on others, an approach that is broadly consistent with Mill's harm principle.[1] To elaborate on that stated in the previous chapter, Mill wrote that 'the principle requires liberty of tastes and pursuits; of framing the plan of our life to suit our own character; of doing what we like, subject to such consequences as may follow: without impediment from our fellow-creatures, so long as what we do does not harm them, even though they should think our conduct foolish, perverse, or wrong' (Mill, 1859/1969, p.15).

However, Mill was not the first of the classical economists to propose something akin to the harm principle. For example, Adam Smith maintained that

> the obvious and simple system of natural liberty establishes itself of its own accord. Every man, as long as he does not violate the laws of justice, is left perfectly free to pursue his own interest in his own way .... According to the system of natural liberty, the sovereign has only three duties to attend to ... : first, the duty of protecting the society from the violence and invasion of other independent societies; secondly, the duty of protecting, as far as possible, every member of the society from the injustice or oppression of every other member of it, or the duty of establishing an exact administration of justice; and, thirdly, the duty of erecting and maintaining certain public works and certain public institutions, which it can never be for the interest of any individual, or small number of individuals, to erect and maintain.
>
> (Smith, 1776/1999, Book IV, pp.273–274)[2]

Again with the addition that it is sometimes legitimate for govern-ments to protect people from harmful behavioural-informed manipu-lations of the exchange relationship (and occasionally to impact on the decisions of people who are influenced by the behavioural phenomena so that otherwise foregone benefits to others might be realised – discussed in greater depth in Chapter 9), the framework proposed in this book is not dissimilar to Smith's.[3]

There are, however, other views, and within behavioural public policy alternative perspectives have thus far dominated. For instance, approaches have been proposed that aim to educate people about the behavioural phenomena that might influence them so that they may, if they choose, make what have been suggested to be more savvy decisions; others aim to foster deliberative decision-making, with the intention that this might reduce reflexive errors. Further approaches call for particular behaviours to be heavily regulated or even, in some instances, banned outright.[4] Still others wish to have a somewhat subtler influence on people, with the objective of enabling them to make better decisions for themselves while at the same time emphasising the importance of individual liberty. It is this last approach, at least in terms of the rhetoric if not always in terms of the application, that has been the most influential conceptual behav-ioural public policy framework to date. All of these approaches will be considered in a little more depth in this chapter, but it seems logical to focus upon the most influential framework first.[5]

PATERNALISTIC YET FREE

The concept of paternalism will be reflected upon in greater depth in Chapter 3, but in a nutshell it is an approach that assumes that those – typically, policy makers – who are targeting others for behaviour change are better at judging what is good for those who are targeted than are the targeted themselves.[6] It is akin to a parent who takes the view that they know what is genuinely good for their children (even if their children might not always agree); hence, the term "paternalism" (i.e. to be paternal). Paternalism thus appears to conflict with liberty.

Yet the thus far most influential behavioural public policy framework purportedly combines both of these concepts, as indicated by its nomenclature, "libertarian paternalism".

Libertarian paternalism was developed by the behavioural economist Richard Thaler and the legal scholar Cass Sunstein (Thaler and Sunstein, 2003, 2008). Like asymmetric paternalism – a similar framework first postulated at around the same time by another eminent group of behavioural economists (Camerer *et al.*, 2003) – libertarian paternalism is a form of means paternalism. Means paternalists believe that people often make mistakes in process – that they do things that, on reflection, they themselves would rather not do, or do not do things that they would rather do. Those who follow libertarian (and asymmetric) paternalism do not wish to be heavily paternalistic with respect to ends – if a person wants to smoke, to avoid physical exercise or to save little for their retirement, for example, there should be no mandatory measures that force them to do otherwise. The reason why people make mistakes, according to the libertarian paternalists, is because of the influence of the so-called behavioural biases.

Thus, like standard rational choice theorists, libertarian paternalists, who have been labelled behavioural welfare economists by Sugden (2018) and behavioural paternalists by Rizzo and Whitman (2020), believe that people ought to want to maximise their utility (or welfare or happiness), but because of the behavioural biases (which are not accounted for in standard economic theory), they often fail to do so.[7] These behavioural biases are the phenomena that behavioural economists and psychologists have observed empirically and that conflict systematically with the assumptions of standard rational choice theory. There is now of course a huge and ever-increasing body of work on the behavioural economic findings, and here is not the place to review them.[8] However, for clarity in going forward in this book, it is perhaps important to state at this point what behavioural economics encapsulates.

There is actually no universally accepted definition of what behavioural economics is, even among behavioural economists.

Some seem to perceive behavioural economics as the study of any and all behaviours relating to economic decision-making, which includes those that are consistent with the standard model of rational choice; others appear to equate behavioural economics with certain psychological phenomena, without making explicit their relevance to economic theory. However, to me, behavioural economics is a set of phenomena that may explain why people's decisions and behaviours sometimes – and in some contexts, often – conflict systematically with the assumptions that underlie the standard economic and rational choice theories.

For example, and at the risk of belabouring the point, independence – an assumption (or axiom) that is central to standard rational choice theory – implies that the value or utility that people assign to any particular outcome will not be influenced by the other outcome(s) to which it is compared. In short, if people are to maximise their expected utility in the standard theoretical framework, then their decisions must not violate independence (and a number of other axioms). And yet in empirical tests and in common observation, we know that this is often not the case. For example, many people are more likely to buy a 48-inch television set for £1,200 than a 44-inch set for £1,000 after a 46-inch set for £1,300 is also included in the choice set. This is because the 46-inch set affects the value that people attach to the 48-inch set, essentially making it appear to offer better value for money than it previously did (see Huber et al., 1982).[9] Other robust behavioural economic findings, at least in particular contexts, are loss aversion and probability weighting (mentioned in Chapter 1), "other regarding" preferences uncovered in trust and social dilemma games as detailed in my Reciprocity book (Oliver, 2019), and present bias (or hyperbolic discounting) – i.e. the observation that people place a heavy emphasis on the "now" and inordinately discount the future.

According to libertarian paternalists, these and other behavioural influences, which they tend to believe are driven by emotions rather than reasoning, are more likely to impact upon fast, automatic, reflexive decisions, rather than slower, more calculative, reflective choices (see Kahneman, 2011).[10] Thus, so their argument goes, people are sometimes – perhaps often – prone to making automatic choices that conflict with what, deliberatively, they would really want to do, when what they really want to do is maximise their utility. Armed with knowledge of the behavioural influences, the libertarian paternalism approach calls for a reshaping of environments – or the "choice architecture" – in which people find themselves, such that automatic choices better align with more reasoned, deliberative preferences. Applications of libertarian paternalism are known as nudges.[11]

For a policy intervention to meet the originally stated requirements of nudging, the intended benefits have to be directed towards those targeted for behaviour change (that is to say, it has to target internalities rather than externalities, the paternalistic arm of libertarian paternalism); it cannot be a regulation or a ban against any particular behaviour (the libertarian arm); and it has to be informed by behavioural science (otherwise it is not part of behavioural public policy). Each of these three requirements is represented by an axis in the behavioural public policy cube depicted in Figure 2.1.

In the cube, movement from north to south on the vertical axis indicates that an intervention is more liberty-preserving than regulatory, movement from east to west on the horizontal axis indicates that the intervention is focused more on addressing internalities than externalities, and movement from south-west to north-east on the diagonal axis indicates that it is informed by behavioural theory rather than standard rational choice theory. A pure nudge would therefore lie at the intersection of the three axes at point A (i.e. a behavioural-informed, liberty-preserving, paternalistic intervention).

When one recognises what the strict requirements of the original formulation of libertarian paternalism are, one has to think quite hard of examples of pure nudges, not least because the lines between rational and behavioural, the extent to which regulation is hard or soft, and whether a policy affects internalities or externalities, are often blurred.[12] However, assuming that some people who automatically choose cheesecake for their lunchtime dessert in their office

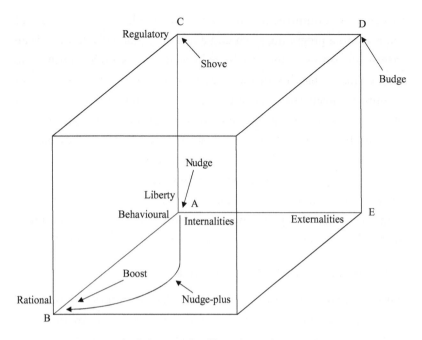

FIGURE 2.1 The behavioural public policy cube

canteen when the cheesecake is salient would, on deliberation, really prefer to eat something healthier but perhaps less salient, like an apple (and that those who choose apples would not deliberatively prefer cheesecake), then a pure nudge might be to place apples at the front and cheesecake at the back of canteen service counters. The positioning of the cheesecake is, as noted, informed by the notion that salience affects automatic decision-making, which renders the intervention behaviourally informed. It is paternalistic in the sense that some of the former cheesecake choosers are now more likely to purchase an item that fits their deliberative preferences better, but nobody is compelled to choose apples, or is denied cheesecake.[13]

One might contend that further examples of pure(ish) nudges are commitment contracts (or, equivalently, deposit or Ulysses contracts) that are sometimes used to try to motivate behaviour change. For example, let us assume that a person deliberatively would like to lose some weight, but his automatic choices often get in the way of this goal. A commitment contract would have him deposit a sum of money into a programme, which he can only gradually retrieve if he meets, for example, his weight reduction targets each month. One may contend that his deliberative preferences imply that the programme is (means) paternalistic, and that the intervention is informed by loss aversion (in that the individual might be particularly motivated by the threat of losing his deposit) – and is thus behaviourally informed.[14] One may also argue that the contract preserves liberty, in that the individual does not have to lose weight if he is not ultimately so inclined; indeed, he does not even have to sign up to the programme in the first place. But is it always obvious that the nudge approach preserves the freedom that is so central to its ethos?

PATERNALISM WITHOUT FREEDOM

If people are not really meant to notice nudge interventions – that is, if nudges change the choice architecture to influence automatic rather than deliberative decision-making – then although some may support their behaviours being influenced as such, presumably there will also be those who as a consequence choose paths that, deliberatively, they would prefer not to take. If so, this approach may be highly statist in some circumstances. Sunstein (2019a) disagrees that nudges are necessarily covert, suggesting that satnavs and road sign warnings – explicit interventions that help people to navigate the world around them – are examples of this instrument. To me, however, satnavs and road sign warnings, in and of themselves, are informational/educational tools rather than behavioural-informed interventions. I am not of course opposed to satnavs and road signs; their use is consistent with Mill's classical liberalism. However, in that they are not necessarily informed by behavioural science, they are not part of behavioural public policy. I therefore have difficulty in defining them as nudges, unless, of course, the design of the information that they convey is in itself informed by behavioural science (and then the *reason* for using particular designs would be, for most people, covert).[15] This latter point in parentheses is important and is worth repeating: a nudge intervention might be physically explicit but is still covert if the reason for its implementation remains hidden from those towards whom it is targeted (which admittedly will not always be the case – for example, the aforementioned commitment contracts).[16]

Nonetheless, Thaler and Sunstein (2008), in addition to insisting that nudges are often overt and explicit, contend that the freedom to choose that they claim is embedded in their framework is the best safeguard against any misguided policy interventions. Indeed, they go further by suggesting that their retaining the notion of liberty not only allows libertarian paternalism to remain in the liberal tradition (Sunstein, 2019a), but that in helping people to satisfy their deliberative preferences, nudges actually enhance freedom (Sunstein, 2019b).[17] However, if we accept that nudges are typically covert instruments, it may be worth noting that Berlin (1969, p.xxxiii), in his introduction to Mill's *On Liberty*, wrote of '[t]he acute consciousness in our day of the dehumanizing effect of mass culture; of the destruction of genuine purposes, both individual and communal, by the treatment of men as irrational creatures to be deluded and manipulated by the media of mass advertising, and mass communication – and so "alienated" from the basic purposes of human beings'. Mill, if he were alive, would likely have been sympathetic to Berlin's concern, which may, if anything, be even more relevant today than at the time that Berlin wrote it, but we may legitimately question whether Mill (or, for that matter, Berlin) would have supported publicly sponsored manipulative countermeasures, with the risk that they may further alienate humans from their "basic purpose" of free and independent thought.

Seemingly somewhat sympathetic to the argument that nudges may undermine the motivation for people to think for themselves, the political scientist Peter John and his colleagues have advocated for the use of interventions that are designed to motivate people to "think", i.e. to encourage people to engage more in deliberative decision-making (John *et al.*, 2011). John (2018) later extended this line of argument by attempting to combine the nudge and think frameworks into one in which people are, in theory, nudged to think (and to think about the nudge that may be before them). John denotes this approach nudge-plus, which calls for an explicit description of the intention of each nudge to be given alongside the intervention. This allows for tests of whether transparency of intention undermines the intervention's effectiveness. For example, in relation to altering the positioning of cheesecake and apples on canteen shelves, a nudge-plus intervention would require a notice to be placed next to the counter explaining exactly why this is done. In Figure 2.1, therefore, a nudge-plus intervention appears to follow the trajectory of the arrow between A and B, perhaps starting off as a classic nudge but by explaining explicitly the reasoning behind the intervention also allows the deliberative self to partake in the final decision.

Another framework called boosting shares some characteristics with John's approach, in that it also focuses on internalities, preserves freedom and attempts to move people towards more explicitly rational decision-making, and is most associated with the psychologists Gerd Gigerenzer and Ralph Hertwig. Like John, the boosters are concerned that nudges, rather than preserving liberty, might to some degree erode individual autonomy.[18] In a defence of nudging, Sunstein (2013) states that, for libertarian paternalists, the term "welfare" refers to whatever choosers think would make their lives go well, which could be elicited via deliberative processes before a nudge is implemented. But even if this definition of welfare is accepted (which, in itself, is consistent with Mill), a nudge can only ever enhance welfare at the aggregate level, because each intervention guides people to go in one particular direction (e.g. in the direction of buying apples rather than cheesecake from canteen counters), which is not consistent with Mill.[19] Moreover, if most people deliberatively decide that they prefer something that the nudger did not a priori accept – e.g. if most people, after deliberating, said that cheesecake is more likely than apples to make their life go well – then it is doubtful that (public sector) nudgers would design and implement interventions in an attempt to move them in that direction. Thus, in nudge policy – understandably, since it is a form of paternalism – there does generally appear to be a pre-decided view held by the nudger on what is good for people in the aggregate, and that deliberative preferences (assuming, of course, that these can be elicited, which, as noted in note 13, is doubtful) are only really used as supporting evidence when they align with that pre-decided perspective.

Since, in reality, nudgers are attempting to change behaviours in ways that they themselves believe improve people's welfare, Hertwig (2017) worries that if the underlying reason for a nudge is not overt, then some – perhaps many – people will be manipulated into doing something that they would prefer not to do. Hertwig thus calls for boost interventions that push people to more explicitly consider their choices by improving their decision-making competencies. According to Hertwig (2017, p.143), '[t]he goal of boosts is to make it easier for people to exercise their own agency in making choices. For instance, when people are at risk of making poor health, medical or financial choices, the policy-maker – rather than steering behaviour through nudging – can take action to foster or boost individuals' own decision-making competences.' He goes on to say that '[r]ather than merely presenting pertinent and accurate information ... boosts explicitly seek to foster existing decision-making competences and to develop new ones, thus enabling individuals to translate their intentions (preferences) into behaviour – that is, to exercise personal agency' (Hertwig, 2017, p.146). Hertwig (2017, p.149) concludes that:

> From the perspective of political philosophy ... many people are not welfarists. Instead, they emphasise the importance of autonomy. Paradigmatic nudges ... and boosts preserve autonomy in the formal sense; they do not prevent people from going their own way. But if autonomy is an important goal and, in particular, if the policy-maker's aim is to promote individual agency, there is an argument in favour of boosts.

Boost strategies can take many forms, but commonly considered ones include teaching people simple accounting rules so as to improve their financial literacy, and instructing them on how to correctly interpret the result of medical tests given the inevitably of false negatives and false positives, so as to offer them an improved understanding of what proportion of those who test positive will actually have the illness under investigation (which may help them in their decision on whether to take the test to begin with, or in their plan of what they will do should they test positive).[20] To summarise, like nudge, think and nudge-plus interventions, boosts focus on the implications for those the interventions target, but they are less paternalistic than nudges because they attempt to educate by enhancing decision-making skills. By improving people's reasoning abilities, but by nonetheless allowing people ultimately, and perhaps more rationally, to choose as they wish, boosts appear to be consistent with Mill's classical liberalism. An effective boost intervention would lie close to point B in Figure 2.1.

From the above discussion it is, I hope, clear that part of the debate between the adherents of the various approaches has focused on the extent to which libertarian paternalism does indeed preserve liberty. However, there is another behavioural public policy approach that frames the preservation of liberty not as a good thing to behold, but as a hindrance. This argument essentially maintains that soft forms of paternalism, by respecting autonomy, are insufficiently effective at altering the behaviours of those who may continue to harm, for example, their own health and financial security.[21] Additionally, it could be contended that think and boost interventions often place too much faith in the competences of people to improve their reasoning skills when making decisions – decisions that can be far more complex than those that humans faced over most of their evolutionary history – even if they are facilitated in these endeavours. The philosopher Sarah Conly has been an active critic of soft paternalism, arguing that over some aspects of personal choice, coercion is warranted (Conly, 2013). The previously discussed approaches are in principle forms of means paternalism – i.e. as aforementioned, they postulate that people are not necessarily making mistakes in relation to where they want to end up (which is often assumed to be the maximisation of welfare or utility), but rather in how they might arrive there; Conly is a means paternalist too, but advocates that in order to overcome people's reasoning failures, more forceful actions are required.

To elaborate a little on this point, Conly (2013) believes that it is often irrational for people to compromise long-term health and financial security by engaging in particular actions (or inactions) that offer short-term pleasures. Specifically, she maintains that if one were to balance broadly defined benefits against broadly defined costs, most individuals would consider it a mistake to smoke tobacco, or to save little for their retirements. Conly contends that, at a societal level, smoking and insufficient saving for retirement cause far more harms than benefits, and the fact that there may be some people who deliberatively prioritise enjoyment in the moment over potential long-term negative consequences does not negate the need for heavy regulation in these areas. In short, over these decisions, Conly sees a heavy emphasis on the immediate moment as a genuine and widespread decision-making error, and thus advocates for a ban on smoking and for mandates that enforce, for many, an increase in savings for retirement.[22] Applications of coercive paternalism, when they are at least in part justified by the possible implications of behavioural phenomena, are called shoves. Like all of the frameworks reviewed above they focus upon internalities, but unlike those other frameworks shoves are highly regulatory. Pure shoves would thus lie somewhere close to point C in Figure 2.1, and are antithetical to classical liberalism.[23]

As noted, all of the approaches discussed thus far in this chapter focus upon addressing internalities, i.e. they are, for the most part, forms of paternalism. Thus, they all target the demand side, i.e. the citizen, the consumer, the patient, etc. They do this to varying degrees of overt and covert, liberty-preserving and liberty-suppressing ways, of course, and it is possible to disagree legitimately over which strategy is the most protecting of individual autonomy, but their shared emphasis is on impacting the demand side rather than constraining the supply side. As discussed briefly in Chapter 1, however, a behavioural public policy framework that is consistent with classical liberalism would require a major emphasis on reducing the harms not that people might impose upon themselves, but on those that some may impose upon others.

PATERNALISM AT ALL?

Paternalism, whether hard or soft, is open to the critique that it unreasonably infantilises the adults it targets, and that policy makers ought to have no role, beyond an openly educative one, in influencing the behaviours of those who are not deemed to lack agency if their activities impose no harms on others.[24] As aforementioned, paternalists in the behavioural field tend to justify their interventions by arguing that people often fail to choose consistently with that which they ought to be doing – i.e. that which maximises their utility; as also noted earlier, whether people indeed ought to be maximising their utility will be scrutinised in some depth in Chapter 4.[25] However, whatever one's perspective is, the infantilising argument presumably holds less force if the objective of a behavioural intervention, or indeed any intervention, is instead to reduce harms that those targeted for behavioural change impose on others.

Sunstein (2019a, p.24) insists that nudges can address externally imposed harms when he writes that '[s]ome nudges are designed to reduce negative externalities, understood as harmful effects on third parties'. Externality-focused nudges have been called "social nudges", and those directed at environmental harms have been labelled "green nudges", but by extending the core term with an ever-increasing use of prefixes in order to account for approaches that were excluded from the original libertarian paternalism framework, there is a danger that every conceivable behavioural-informed policy action will soon be considered, by some, as a nudge of one form or another. If that happens, the approach will be confusing at best, and possibly vacuous. For this reason, it is important to restrict the term nudge to its original intention – specifically, as a particular form of soft paternalism – and to use different terms for manifestly different frameworks.

Fortunately, there is an existing behavioural public policy framework, called behavioural-informed regulation, that focuses explicitly on externalities. Applications of behavioural-informed regulation are known as budges (Oliver, 2013, 2015, 2017). These will form the focus of attention in Chapter 9, and so are mentioned here only in passing, but briefly, they are for the most part a response to a recognition that one party to an exchange may implicitly or explicitly use behavioural insights and, in so doing, cause harms to another party in the exchange. For example, if a lender of a high-interest loan emphasised to potential customers the joys that could be realised through expenditure facilitated by borrowing and at the same time underplayed significantly the monetary liabilities and the consequent longer-term pain of repayment, we might conclude that the lender is using an implicit knowledge of behavioural science – i.e. present bias and salience – in order to manipulate customers to borrow more money than they otherwise would. If so, the principle of a free and fair exchange in this market would have been com-promised, and there is an intellectual justification to regulate the lender's activities. Hence, the budge would be an explicit regulation against a behavioural-informed action that is causing potential harms to others; in their pure form, budges are represented by point D in Figure 2.1.[26]

If you find the concept of budging convincing, then it is possible that you may question whether the most appropriate way forward for behavioural public policy is any form of paternalism. If you are already an anti-paternalist, you might still find budging acceptable. It is important to stress, however, that the different frameworks outlined in this chapter are not necessarily mutually exclusive. Even a fairly committed anti-paternalist might find at least some nudges unobjec-tionable. If it is perceived that a nudge imposes only a small cost on those who, deliberatively, do not want to change their behaviour, then many paternalism sceptics may not object to the intervention. For example, if a person who really prefers to eat a doughnut rather than an apple but who finds himself eating an apple instead due to the deliberate manipulation of item positionings on dessert counters, then even those who question the nudge approach in general might feel that the new apple-eater has been exposed to no serious harms or curtailment of enjoyments, quite aside from the possibility that there might be some worthwhile population benefits from an increase in the consumption of healthy desserts.[27] But many nudges may seriously interfere with personal desires, desires with respect to which – if they impose no harms on others – the policy maker, according to the anti-paternalist, has no business.

As was made clear in Chapter 1, the principal concern of this book is to develop a political economy of behavioural public policy that I will argue has more profound implications than those that have focused on the demand side, and is also more aligned with the values of a liberal society. As part of this effort, Chapter 3 will reflect a little more on whether there are circumstances where paternalism is acceptable and thus may legitimately inform behavioural public policy in ways that my liberal framework cannot.

FOOD FOR THOUGHT

1. Can covert policy interventions preserve individual liberty?
2. Are nudge-plus and boost interventions consistent with promoting independent thought?
3. Is behavioural public policy inevitably paternalistic?

3   A Kingdom of Ends

At a symposium held at the London School of Economics in 2019, several speakers, including Lord Gus O'Donnell, the former head of the British Civil Service under prime ministers Blair, Brown and Cameron, reflected on the content of my *Reciprocity* book. Lord O'Donnell remarked that policy makers are all unabashed paternalists: that they believe that they know better about what is best for people than do the people themselves. This is, in a sense, understandable; for many, that may be the principal reason why they became policy makers in the first place, and for others the culture of the policy-making environment may create, or at least exacerbate, this tendency within them. In short, it appears, to them, that this is what their jobs require them to be. But I am not a policy maker, and I question whether paternalism in policy is an appropriate guiding force.[1]

However, before paternalism can be questioned, we need a clear definition of what it entails. The moral philosopher Gerald Dworkin, in his seminal work on paternalism, defined it as the 'interference with a person's liberty of action justified by reasons referring exclusively to the welfare, good, happiness, needs, interests or values of the person being coerced' (Dworkin, 1972, p.65). Somewhat similarly, Le Grand and New (2015, p.2) contend that 'government intervention is paternalistic with respect to an individual if it is intended (a) to address a failure of judgment by that individual and (b) to further the individual's own good', and they go on to postulate it 'is central to the concept of paternalism that the intervention should be intended to further the good of the person whose judgement or reasoning ability is in question, rather than to further the good of anyone else' (Le Grand and New, 2015, p.16).

If we extend acts of coercion to also include those of manipulation, the definition of paternalism used throughout this book is generally consistent with those stated above, with the exception that the "welfare, good, happiness, needs, interests or values" referred to by Dworkin and the "good" referred to by Le Grand and New is replaced by the "utility, welfare or happiness" of those targeted by government intervention.[2] This is because behavioural welfare economists and others who advocate for paternalism in the field of behavioural public policy, tend often to posit utility, welfare and happiness as interchangeable concepts, the maximisation of which is their normative goal. A paternalistic intervention is thus one that manipulates or coerces an individual into new behaviours with the objective of increasing his utility (or welfare or happiness) over and above that produced by his existing behaviours.

The biggest objection to paternalism is that it undermines individual autonomy. Those who object as such often question why it is allowable for the state to interfere in individual behaviours that impose no harms on others. To understand why autonomy is important in these circumstances we must have an idea of what it means. According to Le Grand and New (2015, p.106), 'autonomous people have the capacity to think, decide, and act for themselves. If we are autonomous, we are the authors of our own lives.'[3] Respecting autonomy thus necessitates that we allow people to live their lives as they see fit (so long as they are not harming others). Immanuel Kant, in kindly offering the title of this chapter, viewed autonomy as of prior importance when he wrote that 'all rational beings stand under the law that each of them should treat himself and all others never merely as a means but always at the same time as an end in himself. Hereby arises a systematic union of rational beings through common objective laws, i.e. a kingdom that may be called a kingdom of ends' (Kant, 1785/1981, p.39).[4] The more contemporary philosopher Joseph Raz (1986) has suggested that viewing autonomy as of ultimate importance – as an end in itself – is a form of paternalism, a somewhat contentious view since respecting autonomy does not equate to manipulation or coercion. It leaves people free to behave in any way they wish.

Openly educating people, so long as it does not indoctrinate nor is deliberately designed to misinform, does not undermine autonomy and is thus not paternalistic either. Indeed, education delivered in this manner – i.e. that which is informed by a neutral assessment of the latest known evidence, reasoned arguments and learning (e.g. smoking increases the risk of lung disease in later life) – enhances autonomy by enabling people to improve their reasoned judgements. Rather, a refusal to educate people with the latest information and knowledge, as well as deliberately misinforming them, may be more paternalistic. Refusing to provide an education was in fact seen as a failure to benefit and, by extension, as a form of harm imposed by some upon others by John Stuart Mill, arguably the most famous anti-paternalist of all.[5]

MILL AGAIN

Mill's antipathy towards paternalism is emphasised in his *Principles of Political Economy*, where he wrote:

> That there is, or ought to be, some space in human existence thus entrenched around, and sacred from authoritative intrusion, no one who professes the smallest regard to human freedom or dignity will call in question: the point to be determined is, where the limit should be placed; how large a province of human life this reserved territory should include. I apprehend that it ought to include all that part which concerns only the life, whether inward or outward, of the individual, and does not affect the interests of others, or affects them only through the moral influence of example.
>
> *(Mill, 1848/1970, p.306)[6]*

On the same page, he went on to suggest that

> it is allowable in all, and in the more thoughtful and cultivated often a duty, to assert and promulgate, with all the force they are

capable of, their opinion of what is good or bad, admirable or contemptible, but not to compel others to conform to that opinion; whether the force used is that of extra-legal coercion, or exerts itself by means of the law.

Although the above, in one sense, underscores Mill's anti-paternalism, that he referred to "force" and "coercion" might, it may be claimed, indicate that Mill was opposed only to hard forms of paternalism (to which, strictly speaking, Mill limited himself in his other writings also). Berlin (1969, p.xvi) believed that Mill had no vision of the types of behaviours that reflect those that behavioural welfare economists believe are irrational today:

> Mill had scarcely any prophetic gift. Unlike his contemporaries, Marx, Burckhardt, Tocqueville, he had no vision of what the twentieth century would bring, neither of the political and social consequences of industrialization, nor of the discovery of the strength of irrational and unconscious factors in human behaviour, nor of the terrifying techniques to which this knowledge has led and is leading.

Nonetheless, the following passage in Mill's *Principles of Political Economy* may offer a reason for libertarian paternalists to believe that he would not have been averse to their vision of soft paternalism:

> To be prevented from doing what one is inclined to, from acting according to one's own judgement of what is desirable, is not only always irksome, but always tends, *pro tanto*, to starve the development of some portion of the bodily or mental faculties, either sensitive or active; and unless the conscience of the individual goes freely with the legal restraint, it partakes, either in a great or in a small degree, of the degradation of slavery. Scarcely any degree of utility, short of absolute necessity, will justify a prohibitory regulation, unless it can also be made to recommend itself to the general conscience; unless persons of ordinary good intentions either believe already, or can be induced to believe, that

the thing prohibited is a thing which they ought not to wish to do. It is otherwise with governmental interferences which do not restrain individual free agency. When a government provides means of fulfilling a certain end, leaving individuals free to avail themselves of different means if in their opinion preferable, there is no infringement of liberty, no irksome or degrading restraint. One of the principal objections to government interference is then absent.

(Mill, 1848/1970, pp.306–307)[7]

From the above, libertarian paternalists might contend that if the behavioural influences drive many people towards ends that they themselves, following a period of deliberation, state that they would prefer to avoid, then so long as the scope to pursue those ends remains, Mill would accept that nobody's freedom has been compromised and an intervention that helps people to satisfy their deliberative preferences is allowable. Of course, we will never really know what Mill's view would have been on this issue, but there is reason to doubt whether he would have supported the use of behavioural insights by the state to manipulate behavioural patterns in particular directions, even if it were the case that those directions aligned with the deliberative preferences of many of those targeted for behaviour change (even if we assume that it is possible to uncover such deliberative preferences). In his *Principles*, he went on to state:

I have reserved for the last place one of the strongest of the reasons against the extension of government agency .... Instruction is only one of the desiderata of mental improvement; another, almost as indispensable, is a vigorous exercise of the active energies; labour, contrivance, judgement, self-control: and the natural stimulus to these is the difficulties of life.

(Mill, 1848/1970, p.312)

Thus, here, once again, Mill expressed a concern that government interventions over individual behaviours risk eroding the capacity for people to think for themselves, placing a significant question mark against the notion that he would have been in favour of a paternalistic reshaping of the choice architecture, even if it is intended to guide people towards actions that many of them might say they prefer to the ones that they habitually choose. Mill would not have wanted people not to have to worry about their own self-control, for example; he would have wanted people to learn to exercise their self-control explicitly and entirely on their own terms. That being said, of the various forms that paternalistic intervention might take, for anti-paternalists (including Mill) soft forms of means paternalism perhaps come the closest to being persuasive.[8] Moreover, as stated in Chapter 2, it is this approach – in the form of libertarian paternalism (at least in terms of the rhetoric) – that has thus far dominated the field of behavioural public policy, and thus we will now consider in a little more depth the paternalistic justifications offered by those who advocate for this approach.

FOUR LIMITATIONS

Le Grand and New (2015) identify four phenomena that they think might distort people's behaviours, choices and actions such that they often fail to end up where they would ideally like to be. They define these phenomena as limited imagination, limited willpower, limited objectivity and limited technical ability, and each, they claim, give the state a justification for paternalistic intervention. Le Grand and New illustrate the limited imagination argument by referring to the tendency for many people to save insufficiently while working to ensure a financially comfortable retirement. Specifically, they write that: 'The best advice on pensions is to begin contributing to a scheme as young as possible: say, before thirty. Yet it is very difficult in one's twenties to imagine oneself in one's sixties or seventies. It is as though one is contemplating a different person: one to whom one has a connection, certainly, but a fairly tenuous one.'[9] Sunstein (2019b) expresses a similar sentiment when he asks us to '[r]ecall that choosers must solve a prediction problem; they must decide, at some point in advance of actual experience, about the effects of one or another option on experience. To solve that problem, knowing "how they feel" is not enough. At a minimum, they must know "how they *will* feel", and they might not know enough to know that.'[10]

Thus, those who believe that limited imagination causes mistakes in people's decision-making invariably contend that state intervention to address these errors is justifiable. As noted earlier in this book, those who advocate for soft forms of paternalism, despite occasional protestations to the contrary, inevitably support measures that are somewhat manipulative (e.g. instituting opt-out as opposed to opt-in pension schemes); advocates of harder forms of paternalism are more open to explicit coercion (e.g. mandating that people invest a minimum percentage of their earnings into a pension plan). One may quite legitimately contend, however, that it is impossible to truly discern whether those who save little for their retirements are genuinely making mistakes in relation to their own personal desires in life. For example, some of these people may have excellent foresight of their future selves and yet still prefer to live in the moment; others might not have, and deliberatively prefer not to have, any foresight of what the future has in store, and are willing to accept whatever life throws at them.

However, Weale, among others – admittedly in relation to the notion of limited willpower rather than limited imagination – has argued that there may be occasions when people would like to be forced away from or towards actions and behaviours that cause harms or benefits to them. Weale (1978, p.162) maintained that: 'Citizens may prefer to be paternalistically coerced if they know they are prone to periodic bouts of weakness of will which allow them to perform actions which they subsequently come to regret.' One could counter this statement by questioning whether the regret that people subsequently come to feel – assuming, of course, that they do indeed actually feel regretful when the reason for regret comes to pass – really does outweigh the benefits that they would have accrued from the behaviours that they are coerced away from. Their later self, even if feeling regretful, may not fully remember – perhaps due to limited imagination – the life that their earlier self enjoyed. This is not to argue that those who wish to be coerced should not be coerced on an individual basis; rather, it is to propose that it is difficult to justify such coercion on the grounds of increasing welfare (or utility or happiness), the normative criteria that most behavioural public policy paternalists implicitly embrace.[11] The coercion (for want of a better term) in this case can, however, be given a non-welfarist non-paternalistic justification if the person to be coerced cannot change his existing behaviours through the force of his own will and has concluded that he would like the state to help him to do so. Here, state intervention to produce behaviour change may not increase the welfare of that individual, but it does respect his autonomy (and strictly speaking, is not, therefore, coercive).

Sunstein (2019a, p.9) takes up the theme of limited willpower (and, implicitly, limited technical ability and limited objectivity also):

> People might have no idea how to get where they want to go.
> Like Adam and Eve, they can be tempted. Sometimes they lack
> self-control. Background conditions greatly matter. Sometimes
> people's choices are not, in the deepest sense, their own; they are
> deprived, deceived, or manipulated. Sometimes they lack crucial
> information. Sometimes their preferences are a product of injustice
> or deprivation. Sometimes they simply blunder. As a result, their
> lives go much worse.[12]

It is difficult to dispute this statement, but one might contend that it offers few grounds for the paternalistic (counter-)manipulation or coercion of citizens. Rather, the concerns may best be addressed by regulating the activities of those who would otherwise manipulate or exploit others, to educate people so that they might better exercise self-control whenever they wish to and so that they are less likely to lack crucial information, and to legislate to address unacceptable injustices and deprivations. Our blunders may serve a useful purpose in incentivising us to think, to reflect and to learn; in short, to help us to develop as human beings.

It perhaps ought to be acknowledged at this point that some view the regulation of those who would otherwise coerce, manipulate or exploit others as a form of indirect paternalism. For instance, Le Grand and New (2015, p.37) comment that:

> Direct paternalism involves only one party, such as prohibiting suicide and drug use; indirect paternalism involves two parties so that the actions of a second person are interfered with to benefit the first, such as laws prohibiting euthanasia or drug sales. In the latter case a restriction is placed on a second party even though the first party has voluntarily entered into an arrangement with the second party that would affect only the first party's interests. The second party may be punished even though it is the first party's (supposed misjudgement) that is being addressed.[13]

However, later in their book, Le Grand and New contend that indirect paternalism, defined as such, is not, strictly speaking, paternalistic at all, because these measures are essentially tackling the harms that one person (or organisation) imposes upon another.[14] In relation to the specific issue of private interests behaviourally manipulating people to act in self-harming ways, Le Grand and New (2015, p.141) note that:

> In these situations neither the private interests concerned nor the government could be said to be acting paternalistically. In the case of the private interests, their intention is not to improve the welfare of the individual but merely to maximize their profits, the effect on the individual being irrelevant [to them]. So, if the effect were detrimental, then government intervention to prevent such would not be paternalistic either but merely intended *to prevent harm to others*; hence it would be an application of the harm principle.

On this, I concur with Le Grand and New.

Placing the above digression to one side, the notion that people have limited objectivity relates to phenomena such as so-called over-confidence bias – i.e. to remind the reader, the tendency for people to be overconfident regarding their abilities, decision-making skills and susceptibilities to life's uncertainties (etc.) – and confirmation bias, or in other words the apparently natural tendency for people to pay most attention to evidence and arguments that support their pre-existing opinions and conclusions. Limited technical ability refers to the difficulties people may face in performing the sometimes quite complicated calculations that are necessary for them to make optimal decisions (from a welfare- or utility-maximising point of view). Taking the four limitations (i.e. those of imagination, willpower, objectivity and technical ability) together, Le Grand and New (2015) conclude that there are two kinds of actions that are most subject to reasoning failure: i) those that may cause harms in the distant future; and ii) those that pose a small chance of an immediate catastrophic outcome. They write:

> These types of activity typically suffer from limited imagination: it is hard to visualize one's future circumstances long into the future, or when the event is very rare. They also are associated with limited willpower – temptation is harder to resist if the benefits from such resistance will not accrue for many years, or if the consequences of a failure to resist seem vanishingly small. And they are linked with limited objectivity – anything risky can be subject to an emotional belief that we are the kind of person that will beat the odds. They may also contain elements of limited technical ability in that a judgment on whether to consume, or to engage in an activity, will involve an accurate assessment of probability, either of an event a long time in the future or of an immediate event with a low probability – something human beings seem quite ill-equipped to do.
>
> *(Le Grand and New, 2015, p.179)*

Le Grand and New are sympathetic to soft forms of means paternalism and particularly to aspects of libertarian paternalism, although the architects of the latter go further with their approach than the two kinds of action summarised in the previous paragraph. Sunstein (2019a), for instance, argues that some construct – i.e. a choice architecture – of the societies in which people live is inevitable with or without government intervention, and will affect people's decisions, an issue that was discussed in Chapter 2.[15] He also contends that since navigability – i.e. the ability for people to choose the best routes for themselves as they sail through life – can pose serious problems for them, it is justifiable for the state to try to ensure that the choice architecture works in people's best interests. Some of those who oppose the preferred nudge strategy of the libertarian paternalists do not deny that individuals might often need help, or protection, with respect to their own behaviours or the behaviours of others. However, as noted earlier, many anti-paternalists believe that attempts to educate people openly about the potential pitfalls they face in life, or to fill gaps in their knowledge, is a more appropriate strategy than reshaping people's environments often without their explicit knowledge, and if others are creating contexts that induce negative externalities then it is legitimate for the state to regulate explicitly against those activities. But those, such as me, who contend as such maintain that we cannot assume that people are harming themselves just because their actions appear to conflict with the tenets of rational choice theory.[16] People may, by and large, be pursuing the lives that they wish to lead (including claiming ownership of their own mistakes and the desire to learn from them), irrespective of how strange their behaviours and decisions might appear from the outside, and if they are imposing no harms on others, the case can be made that they should not be coerced or manipulated into doing otherwise. That is the essence of a liberal society.

THE RETURN TO LIBERALISM

Le Grand and New (2015, p.111) justify their support for soft forms of means paternalism by suggesting that 'if your capacity for autonomy is diminished and you are no longer acting voluntarily, so that the decisions you make and the goals you pursue are not "yours", then an intervention in those decisions does not offend that autonomy – the intervention does not affect the "real you"'.[17] Perhaps unsurprisingly, therefore, towards the end of their book, they pronounce that 'John Stuart Mill was wrong', continuing that 'contrary to Mill's classic statement on the illegitimacy of government intervention to promote an individual's own good ... there are situations where the government should intervene to save people from the consequences of their own decisions, even if no one else is harmed by those decisions' (Le Grand and New, 2015, p.177). As I will argue in Chapter 4, I too believe that Mill was wrong, but not with respect to his views on paternalism.

As already noted, Mill, in his support for educating people so that they are better equipped to lead the lives that they wish to lead, and with his antipathy towards state interference in individual behaviours that impose no harms on others, offers a form of classical liberalism (along with Hume, Smith, etc.) that is reflected in the position taken in this book. Over recent decades, however, in critiquing the school of thought that advocates for minimal state interference and for people to follow their own selfish motivations – an almost libertarian ethos that has been labelled neoliberalism – some have, by association, tarnished the view offered by the classical liberals.[18] Neoliberal thought (and interpretations of it) was perhaps fed by the members of the Austrian School of Economics, who offered a view that was more laissez-faire than that proposed by Mill, although when one studies the Austrian School one realises that the belief system that many of its members shared was also somewhat more nuanced than that suggested by the neoliberal caricature.

Almost eighty years ago, a prominent member of the Austrian School, the economist Friedrich Hayek, expressed qualms with the way in which the concept of liberalism was being misused. He wrote that

> the essential features of individualism which, from elements provided by Christianity and the philosophy of classical antiquity, was first fully developed during the Renaissance and has since grown and spread into what we know as Western European civilisation – the respect for the individual man *qua* man, that is the recognition of his own views and tastes as supreme in his own

sphere, however narrowly that may be circumscribed, and the belief
that it is desirable that men should develop their own individual
gifts and bents. "Freedom" and "liberty" are now words so worn
with use and abuse that one must hesitate to employ them to
express the ideals for which they stood during that period.

(Hayek, 1944/2001, p.14)

He went on to state that:

Because of the growing impatience with the slow advance of liberal
policy, the just irritation with those who used liberal phraseology in
defence of anti-social privileges, and the boundless ambition
seemingly justified by the material improvements already
achieved, it came to pass that toward the turn of the century the
belief in the basic tenets of liberalism was more and
more relinquished.

(Hayek, 1944/2001, p.19)

Hayek was thus clearly frustrated that the term "liberalism" was
being associated with egoistic self-interest. It is important, I think,
to attempt to rescue liberalism from this mischaracterisation, by
emphasising that this approach embodies respect, tolerance and
empathy for all people, and calls for protection against those who
transgress these ideals.[19]

It ought to be admitted, however, that although the members of
the Austrian School shared the view that social cooperation is best
forged by allowing people to be free (and by the operation of a competitive market, which will be discussed in Chapter 7), not all of them
(indeed, perhaps none of them) were as interventionist as Mill with
respect to mitigating harms. Von Mises (1927/2005), for instance, did
not believe in the regulation of personal behaviours that invariably led
to external harms, such as alcohol and drug addictions, because he
was not confident that such policy action would be effective, and,
even if it was, he thought that it could lead to even greater harms.[20]
However, they were explicit in their view that there are some
circumstances in which regulation against certain activities to afford

protection is warranted. For instance, Hayek's fellow Nobel Laureate and Austrian Schooler Milton Friedman and his wife Rose, in a passage reminiscent of one written by Adam Smith (see the beginning of Chapter 2) in their book *Free to Choose*, wished to explore 'how we can limit government while enabling it to perform its essential functions of defending the nation from foreign enemies, protecting each of us from coercion by our fellow citizens, adjudicating our disputes and enabling us to agree on the rules that we shall follow' (Friedman and Friedman, 1980/1990, p.7).

To return to the main focus of this chapter, liberalism and paternalism, despite the invention of libertarian paternalism, do not generally sit comfortably together, but we might yet still ask ourselves whether there are any paternalistic interventions that a Millian liberal would find acceptable, or at least not heavily objectionable.[21]

UNOBJECTIONABLE PATERNALISM?

There are, admittedly, some interventions that are largely justified on paternalistic grounds, and yet which may seem churlish for an anti-paternalist to oppose (for example, the regulations on the wearing of car seatbelts and motorcycle crash helmets mentioned in the endnotes to Chapter 2). This might be the case when the interference with autonomy is minimal, the potential benefits are great and the interventions are not costly to enforce. As Le Grand and New, 2015, p.4) note: 'If a specific means-related paternalistic intervention delivers a large gain in an individual's well-being with only a minor infringement of the individual's autonomy, then the intervention is probably justified; but one involving a small gain in well-being but a severe diminution of autonomy is unlikely to be acceptable.' Similar arguments can be made in relation to some classic behavioural public policy interventions, such as the strategic placement of food items on canteen and supermarket shelves to facilitate healthier choices.

Yet, if justified entirely on paternalistic grounds, I personally remain opposed to coercive and manipulative state interventions, irrespective of how little impact on autonomy their implementers claim them to have.[22] To reiterate, from the outside, how can we really know how intrusive, for everybody, the enforced wearing of seatbelts and helmets or the strategic placement of food items are? For many, they could be very intrusive indeed; for millions, they may be only slightly intrusive, but this will add up to a whole lot of intrusion in the aggregate. Moreover, they might leave some with the uneasy feeling that, although (perhaps) relatively innocuous, such interventions represent an unpalatable thin end of the wedge (see Rizzo and Whitman, 2020, pp.349–397, for an extended discussion of this possibility with respect to manipulation rather than more overt coercion). One may ask, why not just aim to educate people on the pros and cons of their actions and inactions, and then leave their choices to them?

However, as suggested at the outset of this chapter, most policy makers are likely to disagree on this point (and no doubt, on many other points besides). Policy makers are invariably paternalistically inclined, because they tend to believe that people often behave, act, choose and decide in ways that conflict with their own best interests. Thus, it is the policy maker's prerogative – or perhaps duty – to guide, manipulate and even coerce citizens to do better. With paternalistic interventions, so the argument goes, people will experience greater welfare, utility and/or happiness. But should they?

FOOD FOR THOUGHT

1. Is the argument for individual autonomy a form of paternalism?
2. Do humans suffer from limited imagination?
3. Is a regulation against harms paternalistic?

4　The View from Nowhere

The concept of utility, which is treated in this book as interchangeable with welfare and happiness, has a long and confusing history in economics.[1] Indeed, it is among the most confused topics in the history of economic thought. David Hume, one of the earliest writers to use the term utility, seemed to equate it to public usefulness. For instance, in his *An Enquiry Concerning the Principles of Morals*, Hume wrote that: 'In common life, we may observe, that the circumstance of utility is always appealed to; nor is it supposed, that a greater eulogy can be given to any man, than to display his usefulness to the public, and enumerate the services, which he has performed to mankind and society' (Hume, 1751/2018, p.35). Hume went on to argue that the public utility of the social virtues, such as cooperation and reciprocity, is the chief reason from which they derive their merit and natural affection; in short, we approve strongly of actions that are not only useful to ourselves, but are so to others also. Hume saw that type of utility or happiness – i.e. the promotion of the interests of society, which benefits all citizens – as the ultimate goal.

In a later work, Hume refers to the 'happiness of society' as accounting in large part for the origin of morality, and maintains that happiness has three components – action, pleasure and indolence – that exist to differing degrees within different individuals (Hume, 1777/2018, p.188). As noted, according to Hume, our own actions and those of others are driven in the main by a sense of public usefulness, and are undertaken in the pursuit of our own long-term self-interest. In this respect, he suggests that the pursuit of benevolence is consistent with the pursuit of self-love, as is indeed the pursuit of avarice, although avarice is misguided in that it is publicly harmful, and when detected is punished. Happiness, wrote Hume, comes not only with action. Indeed, too much action may be counterproductive; respite is also needed, a sabbath of sorts.

Although pleasure is a part of Hume's schema for happiness (or utility), it is thus just one of three components, with his broader definition offering a rich picture that incorporates prosocial reciprocal actions.[2] However, as suggested in note 2 of this chapter, those more directly associated with utility than Hume – namely, the eighteenth- and nineteenth-century British utilitarians – at least originally restricted themselves to pleasure and the opposite sensation of pain.

HEDONISM AND BEYOND

Jeremy Bentham, widely considered to be the founding father of British utilitarianism, contended that people's actions are governed by (the mental state feelings of) pleasure and pain, which he referred to as the sovereign masters of human behaviour (Bentham, 1781/ 1988). Following this view, these sovereign masters constitute utility. Bentham contended that pleasure and pain are experienced on a con- tinuum and can thus be compared. They guide us on what we ought to do and what we shall do (e.g. eat when hungry, remove our hand from a fire). From this, Bentham derived his famous dictum that societies ought to strive for the greatest happiness of the greatest number, a hedonic calculus that requires the utility that people experience from different possible states of the world to be derived, and that which yields the greatest utility to be pursued. Consequently, utility in this sense has to be cardinal – i.e. the utility index has to reflect the relative strengths of pleasure/pain – and it has to be interpersonally comparable.

It is perhaps needless to say that there have been many chal- lenges to Bentham's utilitarian principle; three of the main points of contention are summarised by Sen (1999). The first concerns the tendency for people to adapt to particular states of the world, which might be especially worrisome in relation to the policies prescribed from the Benthamite calculus if the state in question, by common dispassionate consensus, is adjudged to be bad. Sen refers to this as the happy slave scenario, a term taken from the suggestion that if a slave has adapted to the severe constraints placed upon his freedom and is satisfied with his predicament, then a Benthamite utilitarian would propose that nothing needs to be done to change that person's circumstances (indeed, if such adaptation is a general tendency, then the hedonic calculus might lend support for the introduction and extension of slavery).[3] That would not sit well with the liberal tradition.

The second point of contention is that Benthamite utilitarianism overlooks the importance of addressing inequality. There may be individuals or groups within society who are disadvantaged to the point where, from a social justice perspective, we may wish to target policy action towards them, even if other less disadvantaged groups could experience a greater increase in utility than that experienced by the disadvantaged if they were the target of policy action instead.[4]

Third, there is the deontological challenge to the utilitarian consequentialist view – i.e. that rights rather than outcomes ought to justify policy intervention. For example, all else equal, a lower gain in utility might be expected from a health care intervention that saves the life of a 45-year-old compared to that of a 35-year-old simply due to the fact that, with treatment, the older person has a lower expected number of years of life left, and yet – and again conflicting with the hedonic calculus – it is perhaps likely that there would be broad support for the statement that these individuals have an equal right to treatment.[5]

Sen (1999) contends that rather than attempting to maximise mental state utility within a population, policy makers ought to try to move societies towards a just distribution of basic human functionings (e.g. health, literacy), via equitable access to the capabilities that can help people to achieve those functionings (e.g. decent health care and education services), so that everyone has a reasonable chance to flourish.[6] I too am of the view that the public sector has a predominant role to play in the provision of basic capabilities that cannot efficiently or justly be delivered through private actions, when the outcomes of these capabilities are considered to be of fundamental importance to an individual in the pursuit of his privately held desires, whatever those desires may be. I will return to this issue in Chapter 8.

To be fair to Bentham, he conceived his ideas in the context of the times in which he lived, and observed deep injustices in a British legal system that favoured the titled and entitled and discriminated against the disenfranchised. By advocating for everyone's happiness to be considered equally irrespective of who one was, Bentham was intending to advance, not undermine, the cause of social justice. He also pondered on how utility might be measured empirically, but like the attempt made by the later economist Francis Ysidro Edgeworth to develop a hedonometer, without any success. Nonetheless, his friend, the historian and political economist James Mill, embraced Bentham's ideas, and together they immersed Mill's son, John Stuart, in his school of thought.

Eventually, however, the younger Mill came to believe that the Benthamite restriction on utility to felt pleasure and pain was erroneous; i.e. that it was a mistake to think 'as though [utility] implied superiority to frivolity and the mere pleasures of the moment. And this perverted use is the only one in which the word is popularly known, and the one from which the new generation are acquiring the sole use of its meaning' (Mill, 1863/1969, p.118). In a preamble to his famous line that it is better to be a fool dissatisfied than a pig satisfied (noted in Chapter 3), Mill wrote that:

> Few human creatures would consent to be changed into any of the lower animals, for a promise of the fullest allowance of the beast's pleasures; no intelligent human being would consent to be a fool, no instructed person would be an ignoramus, no person of feeling and conscience would be selfish and base, even though they should be persuaded that the fool, the dunce, or the rascal is better satisfied with his lot than they are with theirs.
>
> (Mill, 1863/1969, p.120)

Mill remained a consequentialist, and did not even abandon utilitarianism (or at least, his own conception of it). One of his most famous works, written after he had moved away from Benthamism, was, after all, titled *Utilitarianism*. However, he did significantly expand the scope of what he believed utility encapsulated, perhaps even beyond that considered by Hume. As suggested by Berlin,

> [Mill] became not so much an open heretic from the original
> utilitarian movement, as a disciple who quietly left the fold,
> preserving what he thought true or valuable, but feeling bound by
> none of the rules and principles of the movement. He continued to
> profess that happiness was the sole end of human existence, but his
> conception of what contributed to it changed into something very
> different from that of his mentors, for what he came to value most
> was neither rationality nor contentment, but diversity, versatility,
> fullness of life – the unaccountable leap of individual genius, the
> spontaneity and uniqueness of a man, a group, a civilisation.
>
> *(Berlin, 1969, p.x)*

In *Utilitarianism*, Mill argued that people should be impartial between their own happiness and that of others, and thus ought to be willing to trade their own for others' happiness if the latter outweighs the former. This suggests that Mill still thought that interpersonal cardinal utility could be adjudged with some degree of accuracy, which at the time that he was writing was a very strong assumption (and remains so today).[7] Moreover, in coming to believe that a selfish concern with one's own feelings of pleasure and pain is an excessively reductive view of what drives, and what ought to drive, human action, whilst at the same time wishing to retain the consequentialist notion of utility, Mill left himself open to the charge of trying to include too many considerations in a single index. For instance, Berlin (1969, p.xiv) thought that the notion of happiness (i.e. utility)

> is "complex and indefinite" in Mill because he packs into it the
> many diverse (and, perhaps, not always compatible) ends which
> men in fact pursue for their own sake, and which Bentham had
> either ignored or falsely classified under the head of pleasure: love,
> hatred, desire for justice, for action, for freedom, for power, for

THE PARETIAN TURN AND THE vNM SIDESTEP 61

beauty, for knowledge, for self-sacrifice. In J. S. Mill's writing happiness comes to mean something very like "realization of one's wishes", whatever they may be. This stretches its meaning to the point of vacuity.

It may indeed be the case that the definition of happiness becomes vacuous if pretty much everything is included within it, but this does not mean that it is vacuous to build a policy framework on the notion that people have diverse desires if it is accepted that the pursuit of happiness does not necessarily drive their desires (on which more later).

By the end of the nineteenth century, most economists and philosophers had resigned themselves to the view that interpersonal cardinal utility is impossible to measure, but most economists, at least, retained the normative assumption that people ought to want to, and indeed, aside from making errors, will, maximise some conception of utility. Since they believed that the measurement of cardinal utility was beyond them, their thoughts turned to a new analytical framework.

THE PARETIAN TURN AND THE vNM SIDESTEP

The birth of modern welfare economics is based not upon cardinal utility, but ordinal utility. That is, all that matters is the direction of preference – i.e. that an individual prefers one thing over another, from which it is implied that the individual gains more utility from the former than from the latter thing in question. The *extent* to which the individual values the former over the latter plays no part in this analysis. Underpinning welfare economics is the concept of Pareto efficiency, named after the Italian economist Vilfredo Pareto, which states that a point of efficiency has been attained if an alternative position cannot make any one person better off without making at least one other person worse off.[8]

As already stated, welfare economics assumes that people ought to, and generally will, seek to maximise utility, and thus in this respect it follows the tradition of classical utilitarianism, but here utility is not observed (or measured, or even defined) directly. Rather, it is inferred from people's choices. The suggestion is that so long as people's preferences are consistent across time and place – i.e. so long as preferences are fixed and stable – then we can assume that these people are maximising utility, given available options and resource constraints. Since utility is undefined, it could mean anything. It could be feelings of pleasure and pain (or even, for a masochist, the pleasure of pain), and thus be Benthamite in nature, but it could encompass what some may see as exotic preferences, such as prosocial concerns and even respect for rights and freedom, which would make it more closely aligned with the views of Hume and Mill. As noted by the economist Kenneth Binmore (2005), in welfare economics it does not matter what people are seeking to maximise, so long as they are seeking to maximise something that maximises their own conception of utility. This widens the scope of the utility function to anything and everything, and thus, as stated by Berlin in relation to Mill's similar conception of utility, as a tool for explanation and prediction the notion of utility in welfare economics is rather vacuous. If, in this framework, people are just required to be consistent in their choices (which can of course be tested), why does utility need to be mentioned at all?

During the early to mid-twentieth century, in parallel with the development of welfare economics, a group of mathematicians and economists were laying axiomatic foundations that culminated in von Neumann–Morgenstern (vNM) expected utility theory (von Neumann and Morgenstern, 1944).[9] vNM expected utility theory is focused on choice in circumstances of risk (and can be extended to include uncertainty); it is the dominant theory of rational choice. If people comply with the axioms of that theory when making their decisions, then this implies that we can use a method – called the certainty equivalence method – to elicit their cardinal utility of the outcomes that they face. With it being developed within the field of economics, the certainty equivalence method was introduced with money as the outcome of interest, but it can (in theory, at least) be applied over any outcome domain.

To illustrate, imagine that an individual is faced with a gamble that offers a 50 per cent chance of winning £100 and a 50 per cent chance of winning nothing. The individual is then required to state the amount of guaranteed money that, for him, would be equally preferable – or in other words he would be indifferent – to the gamble. The guaranteed money amount that he states is his certainty equivalence of the gamble. If the individual does not like risk, he will state a guaranteed amount of less than the expected value of the gamble; i.e. less than £50. Assume that his certainty equivalence is £45. Since £0 and £100 are the worst and best outcomes that he faces in this whole scenario, we can normalise those with utilities of 0 and 1, respectively, on a zero to one index. This then implies that his cardinal utility of £45 is equal to $0.5*1 + 0.5*0 = 0.5$. Through similar processes, one could elicit his cardinal utility of every money amount between £0 and £100 in this example, and by altering the best and worst outcomes in the original gamble one could elicit an individual's utility for larger and even negative money amounts, and indeed for different types of outcomes (e.g. health status, literacy rates etc.).[10]

Like utilitarianism and welfare economics, vNM expected utility theory assumes that people ought to, and, aside from making random errors, will maximise (expected) utility. But again, what type of utility? One might take the view that, as with standard economic theory, utility is in the eye of the beholder, and all that is required is that people be consistent with the expected utility theory axioms. However, given the original construct of the certainty equivalence method (and given that money is invariably used as the outcome of interest), it appears that the focus is on eliciting the relative pleasure that someone would experience from an amount of guaranteed money set against that which they would experience from the possibility of receiving a higher or lower amount. It is true that the purposes for which people would use these money amounts remain unstated, and it is possible that those exposed to the certainty equivalence method may be thinking of using the money for prosocial objectives or for any other aim that requires a financial contribution. However, the narrative that follows vNM expected utility is that people are selfish utility maximisers; indeed, the prosocial choices that are often observed in economic games are typically presented as violations of the assumptions of rational choice theory (i.e. as evidence of economic irrationality).[11] Thus, we might assume that the conception of utility within this approach is generally taken to be consistent with Benthamite hedonic feelings. If so, then perhaps the two most important developments in economic theory over the last one hundred years, and still the dominant frameworks in the discipline today – namely, welfare economics and, in the area of risk and uncertainty, vNM expected utility theory – not only work with different forms of utility (i.e. ordinal versus cardinal), but are also underpinned by different assumptions on what constitutes utility.

As noted, however (and more importantly for our discussion here), welfare economics and vNM expected utility theory do share the notion that people should be consistent in their choices if they are to maximise utility (whatever the definition of utility is). That people are in fact often inconsistent in their choices gave rise to the field of behavioural economics. In the laboratory and in the real world, people's behaviours, decisions and choices are highly context-dependent in ways that cannot be attributed to random error. Humans do not carry an (expected) utility algorithm around inside themselves that is just waiting to be revealed, except perhaps for very simple daily decisions. Nonetheless, most behavioural economists (and particularly those who apply themselves to policy issues) – the so-called behavioural welfare economists and behavioural paternalists – retain the normative postulate of expected utility maximisation.[12] This is why they tend to believe that the common violations of the axioms of vNM theory are systematic biases and errors of judgement. However, again irrespective of what most standard and behavioural welfare economists believe, it may not necessarily be the case that inconsistent choices are tantamount to errors; rather, it might often be the case that people do not want to maximise any notion of utility.[13] Some contemporary economists disagree strongly with this suggestion, yet they do not believe that utility can be inferred accurately from choice. Rather, they aim to define utility more specifically and measure it directly. Unfortunately, the confusion regarding the definition of utility has infiltrated these later economic debates also.

THE NEW ECONOMICS OF HAPPINESS

There are a group of contemporary scholars who continue to believe that all laws and all rules of morality ought to be based on Bentham's greatest happiness principle (e.g. see Layard, 2005). However, as suggested above, methodologically they depart from welfare economics and vNM expected utility because of the evidence that demonstrates that prospective and retrospective evaluations are unreliable indicators of the utility that people will experience, or have experienced in the past (see, for example, Kahneman et al., 1997). These neo-Benthamites thus advocate for a variety of alternative methods that are intended to measure utility more directly, including sliding scales to record the continuous mood of those being assessed, requiring people to record their mental state feelings every minute or so during relatively short episodes, and the day reconstruction method, where people are asked to register their current mood and their activities periodically during the day.

Mood – i.e. mental state feelings of pleasure and pain – initially appeared to be the concern of the neo-Benthamites, and that, as aforementioned, was Bentham's concern also. Recently, however, Layard, along with his co-authors, the economists Paul Frijters, Andrew Clark and Christian Krekel, has written that perception of life satisfaction is currently the best measure of utility because it is less susceptible to the distorting influence that momentary sensations might have on one's view of how happy one is in general (Frijters et al., 2020). Life satisfaction surveys typically ask people to respond on a 0 to 10 scale to the question, "Overall, how satisfied are you with your life nowadays?", with 0 signalling "not at all" and 10 signalling "completely". These surveys do not, therefore, appear to be directly measuring hedonic feelings of pleasure and pain; nor do they correspond exactly to the Aristotelian eudemonic forms of happiness that align to a meaningful, virtuous, worthwhile life, and which might encompass courage, temperance, honesty, benevolence, etc., close perhaps in form to part of Hume's and Mill's notions of utility (Aristotle, 1980). For instance, I might be perfectly satisfied with my life within the rather narrow context in which I live it "nowadays", but if I were to sit down and really think about it, I might recognise that there is no special meaning to my life and that it could be significantly more worthwhile (similar arguments can of course be made with respect to pleasure). This is not to argue at this point that a satisfied life is any better or worse than a meaningful one; it is merely to contend that these two notions of utility differ from one another.[14]

Pleasure, satisfaction and fulfilment are thus different notions of utility, and yet different scholars within the field of economics (let alone outside this field) have different views on what it ought to mean to live a "happy" life. To be fair, it ought to be acknowledged that there are scholars working in the field of happiness studies who explicitly recognise the differences between these various forms of utility, and who advocate for surveys – some of which exist – that try to capture purported measures of each.[15] A possible problem with that approach, however, is that we return to the issue of almost everything potentially constituting utility, and the inevitable trade-offs that would have to be made between the different constituents at the population level may suit few people at the individual level.

Despite the apparent shift in emphasis away from hedonic utility, the neo-Benthamites retain the Benthamite emphasis on (near) experienced utility; i.e. that a close proxy for experienced utility should be periodically measured and aggregated to derive the total value of an episode. However, the claim that an episode – which could be a whole life – can be legitimately valued as such is contentious.

The philosopher Daniel Hausman, for instance, has written that 'a good life is not a sum of the net goodness of its moments .... The same sum of momentary experiences can add up to a wonderful life or an incoherent and mediocre one, depending on how the experiences are ordered and what overall narrative they sustain' (Hausman, 2015, p.114).[16] Following this line of argument, it is the "shape" of an episode – i.e. how the individual moments in an episode fit together – that gives an episode its meaning, and is probably the reason why prospective and retrospective evaluations, the very instruments that the neo-Benthamites distrust, offer a different and perhaps more accurate assessment of the impact that an event may have and/or has had on a person than aggregating the more momentary perceptions.[17]

To return, though, to the definition of utility, and given the above discussion, what should people, and policy makers, be pursuing? Ought people always be consistent in their choices and in what they value? Must all laws and all rules of morality really be based on a single consequentialist principle?

VIEWS FROM EVERYWHERE

Policies that are informed by the postulate of utility maximisation (however utility is defined) are based on population averages – i.e. one pursues policies that produce the highest average utility. However, for many – possibly most – individuals within the population – even if we were to assume that utility is all that anyone cares about – those policy directions that might be optimal on average will be suboptimal for them.[18] The tension between the aggregate and the individual may have been what Hayek had in mind when he wrote that:

> The "social goal", or "common purpose", for which society is to be organised, is usually vaguely described as the "common good", or the "general welfare", or the "general interest". It does not need much reflection to see that these terms have no sufficiently definite meaning to determine a particular course of action. The welfare and

the happiness of millions cannot be measured on a single scale of less and more. The welfare of a people, like the happiness of man, depends on a great many things that can be provided in an infinite variety of combinations. It cannot be adequately expressed as a single end, but only as a hierarchy of ends, a comprehensive scale of values in which every need of every person is given its place.

(Hayek, 1944/2001, p.60)[19]

Thus, Hayek's view on what constitutes welfare and happiness has a flavour of that professed by Mill. Hayek may have been somewhat relaxed about his use of the word "ends", but I would suggest that many, perhaps most, people care also about means (e.g. people care about the rules of the game and a sense of fair play, and not just the final score). I would also contend that a third party (i.e. me, you the reader or a policy maker) cannot possibly discern what each individual wants from life – what drives their decisions and behaviours. People have various and varied legitimate reasons for their actions, both interpersonally and, across context and time, intrapersonally.[20] To assume that (any kind of) utility maximisation is an appropriate universally applicable normative requirement is, according to Sugden (2018), a view from nowhere.[21] As we have seen, over the past 250 years economists have failed to reach an agreement on what utility means even among themselves, which in itself reflects the fact that different people have contradicting views on what characteristics ought to guide human behaviour.

However, ultimately, I suggest that the inconsistences around the definitions of utility – and the fact that there is little empirical support for the notion that everyone wants to maximise utility, whether it be defined in terms of pleasures and pain, general satisfaction or eudaimonia – should not concern us too much, because our normative and descriptive framework ought to be built on something else instead. John Stuart Mill's godson, the philosopher Bertrand Russell, in ruminating on whether utility as pleasure and pain drives people's choices, wrote that:

[I]f what is meant is that, when I desire anything, I desire it because of the pleasure that it will give me, that is usually untrue. When I am hungry I desire food, and so long as my hunger persists food will give me pleasure. But the hunger, which is a desire, comes first; the pleasure is a consequence of the desire. I do not deny that there are occasions when there is a direct desire for pleasure. If you have decided to devote a free evening to the theatre, you will choose the theatre that you think will give you the most pleasure. But the actions thus determined by the direct desire for pleasure are exceptional and unimportant. Everybody's main activities are determined by desires which are anterior to the calculation of pleasures and pain .... Anything whatever may be an object of desire; a masochist may desire his own pain. The masochist, no doubt, derives pleasure from the pain that he has desired, but the pleasure is because of the desire, not *vice versa*

(Russell, 1946/1996, p.745)[22]

Thus, to Russell, desires come first, and desires are many and varied and differ across people (although some "basic" desires – such as the desire to be fed, sheltered, free of physical and mental suffering, etc. – are almost universal, because they help to support the pursuit of the less basic person-dependent desires).[23] Everyone has desires, which could include the desire for pleasure, to be publicly useful, to be generally satisfied, or to assign some sense of worth to one's life, but may also include the desire to feel nothing or to do nothing, to be solitary, to renounce ambition, to never search for meaning, to always keep one's promises, to be true to oneself irrespective of the personal and professional consequences, or even to write books that hardly anyone will ever read (among countless other desires). To me, this viewpoint is compelling: it allows people to pursue any of the various types of utility that have been favoured by different scholars through-out the history of economic thought if they so wish, but it also allows people to seek to satisfy any other desire that they might have instead.[24] Paternalism in the form of manipulating or coercing people towards particular ends has no place in this framework; policy makers, at least in the realm of personal lifestyle choices, must limit themselves to providing the general conditions that might best help people to lead their lives – to follow their desires – as they themselves see fit. It is a framework that facilitates the desired life.

A SHORT SUMMARY

I hope I have conveyed in this chapter that discussions on utility in the history of economic thought have been complex and confused. My review of that history, due to space constraints, has been somewhat fleeting, but in an attempt to further clarify can be summarised as follows.

In the latter part of the nineteenth century, most mainstream economists turned away from the utilitarian dream of measuring cardinal utility, believing such a task to be impossible. Modern welfare economists instead proposed consistency requirements for individual decision-making. The composition of utility went unstated; so long as people were consistent in their choices, it was assumed that they would be maximising whatever individually gave them the most utility. vNM expected utility theory, developed in the mid-twentieth century, offered the tools to measure cardinal utility, but in order for the theory to "work", in common with standard welfare economics, it required people to be consistent with a set of axioms when making their choices.

In the second half of the twentieth century, behavioural economists and psychologists discovered that people often systematically violate those axioms. In short, people are frequently *in*consistent in their choices. Rather than perceiving that there may be something wrong with the normative objective of utility maximisation embedded in standard economic theory and rational choice theory, however, most behavioural economists, and in particular those who have been especially engaged in policy applications (i.e. the behavioural paternalists), took the view that people are often mistaken, erroneous and biased in their choices. Consequently, the dominant behavioural public policy frameworks to date call for policy makers to aim to correct these biases, so that people are more likely to maximise their welfare.

The neo-Benthamites of the early twenty-first century also recognise that there are inconsistencies in choice behaviours, but in order to take us "back to Bentham" – i.e. to reignite his dream of introducing policies to secure the greatest happiness in a population – they contend that utility needs to be better defined and measured, and that choice-based measurement tools ought to be discarded. The neo-Benthamites argue for the use of direct measures of mood, life satisfaction and eudemonia. The trouble is – without even listing most of the criticisms that have been waged against the original form of utilitarianism – the neo-Benthamites have not yet settled on what happiness (or utility) is, and whatever it is, choosing policies that produce the greatest average level of population utility are likely to generate a whole lot of individual misery. To give a hypothetical example, if it were discovered that married persons are, on average, happier than the unmarried, and that the childless are, on average, happier than parents, then a social planning utilitarian might advocate for policies that incentivise marriage and disincentive pregnancy. As such, public resources would be directed towards incentivising a great many individuals to do things that conflict with their own individual desires in life.[25]

Of course, the framework that I am proposing in this book acknowledges the systematic inconsistencies in choice behaviours, but attributes much of the concern regarding these to a mistaken normative adherence to utility maximisation. If a person's consideration of some monistic overarching sense of utility does not precede the choices that he makes – if instead his personal desires are legitimately driven by a host of context-dependent value judgements – then why would, or should, he be consistent with respect to the aggregation of a particular type of outcome that is, at best, of secondary importance to him?[26] People, I contend, have their own personal desires that vary interpersonally and intra-personally across context, but cooperative, reciprocal actions with their fellow citizens can facilitate people in the pursuit of most of their desires, whatever those desires may be. I suggest that the role of the policy maker is thus to nurture those reciprocal instincts.

FOOD FOR THOUGHT

1. Is the pursuit of pleasure humankind's most important objective?
2. Are interpersonally comparable cardinal utilities measurable?
3. Do considerations of utility precede desires, or vice versa?

5 Nourishing Flourishing

As will be clear from Chapter 4, it is my contention in this book that what ought to drive human actions and behaviours should not be reduced to a single outcomes-based maxim. If one accepts this argument, it cannot therefore follow that people ought to be manipulated or coerced towards behaving and thinking in accordance with any monistic objective. There are parallels here with Hayek's concerns in *The Road to Serfdom*, in which he maintained that:

> The desire to force upon the people a creed which is regarded as salutary for them is, of course, not a thing that is new or peculiar to our time. New, however, is the argument by which many of our intellectuals try to justify such attempts. There is no real freedom of thought in our society, so it is said, because the opinions and tastes of the masses are shaped by propaganda, by advertising, by the example of the upper classes, and by other environmental factors which inevitably force the thinking of the people into well-worn grooves. From this it is concluded that if the ideals and tastes of the great majority are always fashioned by circumstances which we can control, we ought to use this power deliberately to turn the thoughts of the people in what we think is a desirable direction. Probably it is true enough that the great majority are rarely capable of thinking independently, that on most questions they accept views which they find ready-made, and that they will be equally content if born or coaxed into one set of beliefs or another. In any society freedom of thought will probably be of direct significance only for a small minority. But this does not mean that anyone is competent, or ought to have power, to select those to whom this freedom is to be reserved. It certainly does not justify the

presumption of any group of people to claim the right to determine
what people ought to think or believe.

(Hayek, 1944/2001, pp.168–169)[1]

In short, people have desires that are personal to them, and so
long as they are not harming others it is not the business of third
parties, including policy makers, to manipulate or coerce them in
the direction of, for example, utility maximisation, because many –
perhaps most – people may not be principally driven to maximise
utility (even if there were a commonly agreed upon notion of what
is meant by utility). It seems reasonable, however, to accept that
most of the time people have a personal objective or objectives that
underpin their desires, whether they be outcomes-driven (e.g. good
health), process-driven (e.g. promises kept) or a bit of both. To
reiterate, privately held desires are person-specific (and range from
a desire to do nothing to being driven to provide for one's family to
aspiring to become a prime minister or a president), although many
people will of course have similar or even shared desires.
Nonetheless, a common term for the achievement of one's desires,
irrespective of what those desires may be, is convenient for my
exposition, and the term used here is "flourish". Thus, a person
has a desire to flourish, and the attainment of one's desires is
indicative of a flourishing life.[2]

The suggestion that people have their own personal multifarious desires in life at which no third party would be adept at second-
guessing was not lost on many of the utilitarians. For example, the
utilitarian philosopher Henry Sidgwick wrote that 'men, on average, are more likely to know what is for their own interest than
government is' (Sidgwick, 1891, p.37), and Mill, in *On Liberty*,
maintained that:

> If it were felt that the free development of individuality is one of the
> leading essentials of well-being; that it is not only a co-ordinate
> element with all that is designated by the terms civilisation,
> instruction, education, culture, but is itself a necessary part and

condition of all those things; there would be no danger that liberty should be undervalued.

(Mill, 1859/1969, p.55)

He went on: 'Human nature is not a machine to be built after a model, and set to do exactly the work prescribed for it, but a tree, which requires to grow and develop itself on all sides, according to the tendency of the inward forces which make it a living thing' (Mill, 1859/1969, p.57).[3] Thus, I do not disagree with those utilitarians (and later welfare economists) who were of the view that people have varied plans for their lives that outsiders should normally not seek to override; but as will by now be clear I disagree with their contention that the expectation of utility necessarily drives human behaviour. This, as I have tried to explain earlier, is important for behavioural public policy, because accepting that desires are antecedent leads to the conclusion that outcomes-based inconsistencies in decision-making – i.e. the empirical findings in behavioural economics – are not necessarily indicative of human error.

There is a further assumption underpinning rational choice theory that conflicts with the thesis of this book, an assumption that is often somewhat unfairly ascribed to all branches of utilitarianism and to welfare economics also; that is, that people are necessarily motivated by selfish self-interest, or egoism. The confusion around what is meant by utility has not helped in the tarnishing of all of these branches of economics with the same brush in this respect. Liberalism is sometimes similarly maligned by those who associate it with the selfishness that underpins neoliberalism. It might therefore prove instructive to outline briefly the key premises and components of the welfare economic and liberal economic traditions.

SOME PREMISES AND COMPONENTS

According to Bernheim (2016) there are three general premises of standard welfare economics. The first is that each of us is the best judge of our own welfare, which, as noted in Chapter 4, can include anything, including prosocial concerns. The second premise is that our judgements are governed by coherent, stable (consistent) preferences, and the third is that our preferences guide our choices, and when we choose, we seek to benefit ourselves (which, if you are prosocially motivated, will benefit others also). In welfare economics, therefore, the source of utility can vary across people, and there is no assumption that people are necessarily selfish egoists. There are some similarities – but also some differences – here with the assumptions that underlie the liberal economic tradition that predates modern welfare economics.

Sugden (2018) identifies what he sees as three key components held in common across the liberal tradition of economic thought (i.e. that created and followed by Hume, Smith, Mill, the Austrian School, etc.).[4] The first is that in a well-ordered society, cooperation for mutual benefit should be a principle that governs all aspects of social and economic life. The second is the assumption that the competitive market is a network of mutually beneficial transactions, and competitive markets belong to the class of institutions in which individuals cooperate for mutual benefit. Finally, and in common with welfare economics, it is assumed that each individual is the best judge of what counts towards his benefit, and thus there ought to be no paternalistic interventions by government authorities.[5]

Therefore, following Sugden and as intimated earlier in this book, mutuality, reciprocity and cooperation are emphasised in the liberal economic tradition as being important tendencies in order for people to get what they individually may want. Sugden's liberal components are vague on whether individual choices are driven by the desire to maximise some notion of utility – i.e. on "what counts as his benefit". Sugden himself does not think that utility maximisation is necessarily the motivator of individual choice, but it seems uncontroversial to state that most of the prominent liberal economic thinkers throughout history did believe that the expectation of experiencing some conception of outcomes-based welfare, happiness or utility is a principal causal explanation for individual action. However, consistency in preferences across different contexts does not seem to be a fundamental requirement in the liberal tradition (as it is in welfare economics), lending scope for people to value particular things differently in different circumstances; that is, preferences are allowed to be context-dependent, a viewpoint that might see nothing inevitably erroneous in many of the findings that have been uncovered by modern behavioural economists. Placing most of these differences and similarities between the liberal tradition and welfare economics to one side, however, my exposition at this point requires a return to the first point raised; namely that liberal economists believed that people are, and ought to be, driven to cooperate by the prospect of personal benefit.

AGAINST EGOISM

Those who advocate that people ought to be motivated by selfish egoism in their economic decision-making often appeal to Adam Smith's notion of an invisible hand forging efficiency in the market, and even to Charles Darwin's theory of natural selection, where one should supposedly applaud the survival of the fittest in a dog-eat-dog world.[6] However, as I argued in my *Reciprocity* book, a close reading of Smith's (1759/2009) *The Theory of Moral Sentiments* ought to lead one to recognise that his views on what does and should motivate human behaviour is a lot more nuanced than that which is often credited to him. Smith actually maintained that reciprocity, both in the positive and, particularly, negative senses of returning good and bad intentions and actions in kind, is crucial to the proper functioning of society, and is perhaps of paramount importance in economic exchange also, once one goes beyond the trade in simple goods to those where there are substantial market failures (e.g. asymmetries in information between buyers and sellers).[7]

Darwin's views, when being used as a justification for selfishness, are also often misrepresented. The historians James Moore and Adrian Desmond tried to set the record straight in their introduction to Darwin's *The Descent of Man*, where, in relation to hunter-gatherer societies, they wrote that 'the notion of harmony *within* each tribe – rather than competition – would be factored into the *Descent* to explain the emergence of morality and compassion, for [Darwin] the highest human attributes. Clearly, among competing tribes, those with most moral and altruistic members had won out, so there must be a social value to sympathy and selflessness' (Moore and Desmond, 2004, p.xxxix). One might wonder how a person who gives unconditionally could possibly have an evolutionary advantage; Moore and Desmond (2004, p.xl) go on to state that:

> Even [Darwin] wondered how altruists could survive to leave more offspring (the test of "fitness"), when they were, by definition, more vulnerable. In this he raised the modern dilemma of evolutionary biology. Darwin actually anticipated a later solution by mooting a form of "reciprocal altruism", where do-gooders would "receive aid in return" and this would strengthen the cohesion of the group.

To turn to Darwin explicitly, he wrote that 'certain mental powers ... have been chiefly, or even exclusively, gained for the benefit of the community, and the individuals thereof, have at the same time gained an advantage indirectly' (Darwin, 1879/2004, p.83), and that:

> With mankind, selfishness, experience, and imitation, probably add ... to the power of sympathy; for we are led by the hope of receiving good in return to perform acts of sympathetic kindness to others; and sympathy is much strengthened by habit. In however complex a manner this feeling may have originated, as it is one of high importance to all those animals which aid and defend one another, it will have been increased through natural selection; for those communities, which included the greatest number of the most sympathetic members, would flourish best, and rear the greatest number of offspring.
>
> *(Darwin, 1879/2004, p.130)*

Those who support what has become known as neoliberalism, in common with the classical liberals, place a heavy emphasis on individualism and freedom, but the former have caricaturised the arguments made by the latter to justify egoism in human actions and behaviour, representations that, as the preceding paragraphs briefly highlight, are often misleading.[8] That said, the contention that individualism breeds selfishness is not new. For example, de Tocqueville, who contended that democracy incentivises individualism in his studies of America, noted that: 'Feelings and opinions are recruited, the heart is enlarged, and the human mind is developed only by the reciprocal influence of men upon one another. I have shown that these influences are almost null in democratic countries; they must therefore be artificially created, and this can only be accomplished by associations' (de Tocqueville, 1835/1998, p.218).[9] The erosion of the natural ties that held people together in nineteenth-century America, according to de Tocqueville, was the catalyst for the creation of an unprecedented number of societies and associations, as people sought substitutes for the relationships that had previously been taken for granted.

However, to elaborate, the liberal economists did not believe that individualism causes selfishness; indeed, quite the opposite.[10] For instance, Hayek (1944/2001, pp.62–63) maintained that

> individualism ... does not assume, as is often asserted, that man is
> egoistic or selfish, or ought to be. It merely starts from the
> indisputable fact that the limits of our powers of imagination make
> it impossible to include in our scale of values more than a sector of
> the needs of the whole of society, and that, since, strictly speaking,
> scales of value can exist only in individual minds, nothing but
> partial scales of values exist, scales which are inevitably different
> and often inconsistent with each other. From this the individualist
> concludes that the individuals should be allowed, within defined
> limits, to follow their own values and preferences rather than
> somebody else's, that within these spheres the individual's system
> of ends should be supreme and not subject to any dictation by
> others .... This view does not, of course, exclude the recognition of
> social ends, or rather a coincidence of individual ends which makes

it advisable for men to combine for their pursuit. But it limits such common action to the instances where individual views coincide; what are called "social ends" are for it merely identical ends of many individuals – or ends to the achievement of which individuals are willing to contribute in return for the assistance they receive in the satisfaction of their own desires. Common action is thus limited to the fields where people agree on common ends. Very frequently these common ends will not be ultimate ends to the individuals, but means which different persons can use for different purposes. In fact, people are most likely to agree on common action where the common end is not an ultimate end to them, but a means capable of serving a great variety of purposes.

On this view, which more or less concurs with that which I have heretofore been postulating, a liberal accepts that desires generally vary across people, but that people cooperate in the pursuit of their own individual desires, and in some cases they cooperate to achieve a commonly held end, an end that tends to facilitate their pursuit of a flourishing life irrespective of what their individually held desires may be (a point to which we will return in Chapter 8).

That social cooperation thrives in a free society was a view shared widely among the members of the Austrian School of Economics. For instance, von Mises, with echoes of Smith, began his book, *Liberalism*, with the statement that:

Human society is an association of persons for cooperative action. As against the isolated action of individuals, cooperative action on the basis of the principle of the division of labor has the advantage of greater productivity. If a number of men work in cooperation in accordance with the principle of the division of labor, they will produce (other things being equal) not only as much as the sum of what they would have produced by working as self-sufficient individuals, but considerably more. All human civilization is founded on this fact.

(von Mises, 1927/2005, p.1)[11]

In short, many of those who follow the classical liberal economic tradition suggest that left to their own devices, people will, and should, cooperate and reciprocate for the good of all those involved, driven by the individual pursuit of their own desires.[12] However, some scholars who can also be classified as liberals in the sense that they strongly support the notion of freedom, are less convinced that people's cooperative tendencies will always sufficiently shine through, and therefore that public policy makers should focus upon attempting to take advantage of other human motivational forces. For instance, Le Grand (1997) maintains that public sector professionals are motivated substantially by egoism, and thus institutional arrangements ought to be designed so that their fundamental tendencies in this regard are directed towards incentivising them to deliver good-quality services (e.g. school administrators and teachers ought to have to compete for budgets and pupils so as to encourage them to provide a high standard of education), and Thaler and Sunstein, of course, believe that people will often be led astray by the behavioural influences (which might reasonably include a lack of engagement in personally beneficial cooperative activities) unless their environment is specifically designed to motivate them to do otherwise.

While recognising that people are often motivated by many factors, including egoism and perhaps even occasionally pure altruism, the reader will by now be aware that I align with the classical liberals in believing that considerations of reciprocity are a core driver of human actions and behaviours that evolved for the reasons specified above.[13] Moreover, as stated in Chapter 4, over private actions, unlike the libertarian paternalists (or indeed, any paternalists), I cannot conclude that people are in error just because, from an outside perspective, they appear to be doing something odd. Thus, with respect to personal lifestyle choices, I do not believe that policy makers ought to manipulate or coerce people to act and behave in ways that the policy maker deems fit, assuming, of course, that they are not substantively harming others. However, since reciprocity is a powerful motivational force for benefiting individuals and the groups to which they belong, it is beholden on policy makers to attempt to nurture this human tendency, and certainly to attempt to prevent it from being crowded out, so as to give citizens ample opportunity to flourish on their own terms.

NURTURING RECIPROCITY

The historian Helena Rosenblatt (2018) points out that classical Greek and Roman thinkers regularly emphasised the importance of mutual helpfulness in sustaining a free and generous society, and thus the classical liberals were on to nothing new in that regard. But de Tocqueville (who, admittedly, at times is a little self-contradictory) iterated this sentiment in his detailed study of an actual society when he wrote that:

> The free institutions which the inhabitants of the United States possess, and the political rights of which they make so much use, remind every citizen, and in a thousand ways, that he lives in a society. They every instant impress upon his mind the notion that it is the duty as well as the interest of men to make themselves useful to their fellow creatures: and as he sees no particular ground of animosity to them, since he is never either their master or their slave, his heart readily leans to the side of kindness. Men attend to the interests of the public, first by necessity, and by dint of working for the good of one's fellow citizens, the habit and the taste for serving them are at length acquired.
>
> *(de Tocqueville, 1835/1998, p.213)*

Reciprocity and liberty are thus mutually reinforcing. However, returning to the Romans (or thereabouts) once more, Edward Banfield (1958), in his immersive study of a poor rural Italian region in the 1950s, found that a community spirit – a mutuality of interests – can, unless one is careful, be almost entirely crowded out.[14]

Reciprocal and cooperative tendencies have to be protected and nurtured. Mill (1863/1969, p.121), with his fondness for horticultural analogies, wrote that the:

Capacity for the nobler feelings in most natures is a very tender plant, easily killed, not only by hostile influences, but by mere want of sustenance; and in the majority of young persons it speedily dies away if the occupations to which their position in life has devoted them, and the society into which it has thrown them, are not favourable to keeping that higher capacity in exercise.

In my *Reciprocity* book I offered a fairly detailed exposition of the importance of reciprocity and how it might be nurtured, but since motivating reciprocity is an important component of the political economy of behavioural public policy that I am proposing here, for the remainder of this chapter it might be instructive if I cover some of that same ground again. To that end, three general recommendations are offered: that reciprocity be emphasised in the political and policy rhetoric; that the concentrations of income and wealth into the hands of a small percentage of any given population be addressed; and that policy decision-making be decentralised.

The Importance of the Message

In order to encourage people to act and behave reciprocally in both their private choices and in relation to any decisions that fall within the realm of public policy, it is important that politicians and others in positions of authority give the impression that they genuinely believe that practicing reciprocity has positive implications. Relatedly, de Tocqueville (1835/1998, p.246) wrote that 'the sole effectual means which governments can employ in order to have the doctrine of immortality of the soul duly respected is always to act as if they believed it themselves'. Messages that proclaim that "greed is good" or that "there is no such thing as society" can have a powerful influence in bringing to the fore aspects of human nature that crowd out those which might better serve the social interest, and by extension people's long-term self-interest; it would be wise for political leaders to recognise this and to frame their messages accordingly.

The Importance of Fairness

Regarding the social circumstances of the late nineteenth century, Rosenblatt (2018, p.266) states that

> a growing number of British liberals began to favour a new type of
> liberalism that advocated more government intervention on behalf
> of the poor. They called for the state to take action to eliminate
> poverty, ignorance and disease, and the excessive inequality in the
> distribution of wealth. They began to say that people should be
> accorded not just freedom, but the conditions of freedom.[15]

All of this is important and relates directly to the view that a certain level of income is a basic capability that is foundational to the capacity to flourish as a human being, irrespective of one's desires (cf. Sen, 1999). However, for here I wish to focus upon the concern regarding an 'excessive inequality in the distribution of wealth', which is not restricted to the claim that people should have enough to fulfil their desires (an absolute argument), but also considers perceptions of what is fair (a relative argument). If a sufficient number of people perceive a basic unfairness in how society is organised and structured, or in how the economy operates, then the incentive to behave cooperatively – to reciprocate (other than perhaps in the negative sense of wishing to punish those that are perceived as the agents and/or profiteers of unfairness) – might be undermined to an extent that causes significant social harm. As Banfield (1958) observed, when life appears hard and unfair (which resonates with the arguments pertaining to behaviour in the face of extreme scarcity, rehearsed in Chapter 1), people tend to retreat into themselves.

However, liberals have long contended that not all inequality in income or wealth is necessarily bad, since a degree of inequality may serve as an engine for aspiration and growth (e.g. von Mises, 1927/ 2005). For instance, partly on these grounds, Friedman and Friedman (1980/1990) saw the decision to impose taxes on the highest earners in society so as to help financially those at the bottom as entirely antithetical to liberty. Many might be of the view that the position advocated by Friedman and Friedman in this respect is closer to egoistically driven neoliberalism than cooperative liberalism, but to give them the benefit of the doubt, they were writing (just) before the onset of the substantial increases in income and wealth concentrations in the hands of small percentages of the population witnessed in many countries over the past few decades. For example, the charitable confederation Oxfam (2017) reported that the wealth now owned by the eight richest people in the world is equivalent to that owned by the poorest 50 per cent, and the economists Lawrence Mishel and Natalie Sabadish noted that by 2012 a typical American chief executive officer earned 354 times more than the average worker, up from only 20 times more 50 years ago (Mishel and Sabadish, 2013).[16] These developments may well be a substantive challenge to the natural tendency for people to reciprocate and cooperate, for a number of reasons. For instance, if a small number of people are able to harvest off for themselves a high and increasingly disproportionate share of the income and wealth that a society creates, it might undermine for some the notion that cooperative endeavour breeds individual reward (i.e. it may serve to disillusion some regarding the potential benefits of cooperation); for others, it might serve as a signal that it is acceptable – or even aspirational – to be selfish.

The concentration of too much income and wealth – and accompanying power (which undermines democracy, if power principally resides with the unelected super-rich) – within a small percentage of the population is antithetical to the promotion of liberty within society as a whole, both in the absolute sense of far more people otherwise having access to resources that could facilitate their own conceptions of what it means to flourish, but also, as I have argued here, in a relative sense – in the sense of the perceptions that this state of affairs has created around how one should treat one's fellow citizens.[17] Some inequality is very likely to be necessary and desirable to incentivise human aspiration and growth, but too much income and wealth concentration undermines the motivations that facilitate human flourishing and has been allowed to develop into one of the defining problems of our age.

The Importance of Local Autonomy

The importance of the message and of fairness are both principally, although not entirely, mentioned in relation to encouraging reciprocity in people's private actions. In this final category, which argues for a decentralisation of public policy decision-making, the emphasis is on the behaviours of public sector professionals. The decentralisation of the management of public sector services to local planners, purchasers and providers has a lot to commend it. For example, securing reciprocal motivations and actions and abating egoistical ones is more difficult the larger the group. Also, a decentralised approach affords greater local level innovation, which, if good results were shown, could be disseminated cross-regionally (I will return to this point below). Moreover, local-level actors are likely to be more in tune with, and more responsive to, the objectives and priorities of the people they serve.[18]

Hayek (1944/2001), in critiquing the central planning of a manu-facturing sector, argued that as the factors that have to be taken into account become so numerous, it becomes impossible to obtain a synoptic view of them, and thus decentralisation becomes necessary. Similar arguments could be made with respect to the provision of public sector services, but decentralisation in these sectors does not entail the devolvement of all public policy decision-making to the local level. To return once again to Mill (1859/1969, p.105):

> Government operations tend to be everywhere alike. With
> individuals and voluntary associations, on the contrary, there are
> varied experiments, and endless diversity of experience. What the
> State can usefully do is to make itself a central depository, an active
> circulator and diffuser, of the experience resulting from many trials.
> Its business is to enable each experimentalist to benefit by the
> experiments of others; instead of tolerating no experiments
> but its own.

If we substitute local decision-making bodies – e.g. local and regional councils, or even local schools, hospitals, etc. – for the 'individuals and voluntary associations' in the above passage, then there is consistency with Mill's views if we contend that local officers and professionals ought to have a great deal of freedom with respect to managing the provision of public sector services, and should only be held to account by the central state regarding their compliance with general laws, regulations and requirements. Although Mill argued that it is the role of the central state to denounce those who transgress the general laws and regulations, a more concentrated imposition of its will on the localities will result in the latter becoming docile and incapable of achieving anything of note. If, however, local decision-makers are given the freedom to innovate, then the central state can also assume the function of disseminating good practice throughout the whole of a country (and perhaps beyond) – in other words, to become the active circulator and diffuser that Mill imagined.[19]

To conclude this chapter, I have argued that people have desires, the fulfilment of which results in their own conception of a flourishing life (which, from individual to individual, may or may not have anything to do with any of the various conceptions of utility). Policy makers can nurture the conditions by which people might have the best chance of fulfilling their desires; conditions which, ideally, protect and foster the intrinsic human tendency to reciprocate. However, one should not try to force people to be cooperative; the tendency to reciprocate ought to be autonomously driven, and the extent to which people are driven to reciprocate – both positively and negatively – will often be influenced heavily by perceptions of desert.

FOOD FOR THOUGHT

1. Is it acceptable to have a desire to do nothing with one's life?
2. Is freedom the best means by which to motivate cooperative actions?
3. How might the reciprocal instinct be crowded out?

6   Anyone for Desert?

In his classic book *Doing & Deserving*, Joel Feinberg posed the following question: 'What is it to deserve something? This guileless question can hardly fail to trouble the reflective person who ponders it. Yet until its peculiar perplexities are resolved, a full understanding of the nature of justice is impossible, for surely the concepts of justice and desert are closely connected' (Feinberg, 1970, p.55).

Many earlier philosophers would not have disagreed. In the *Nicomachean Ethics*, for instance, Aristotle wrote that 'awards should be "according to merit"; for all men agree that what is just in distribution must be according to merit in some sense' (Aristotle, 1980, p.112). In *An Enquiry Concerning the Principles of Morals*, Hume stated that:

> When any man ... renders himself by his crimes obnoxious to the public, he is punished by the laws in his goods and person; that is, the ordinary rules of justice are, with regard to him, suspended for a moment, and it becomes equitable to inflict on him, for the *benefit* of society, what otherwise he could not suffer without wrong or injury.
>
> *(Hume, 1751/2018, p.16)*

And in *Utilitarianism*, Mill contended that:

> [I]t is universally considered just that each person should obtain that (whether good or evil) which he *deserves*; and unjust that he should obtain a good, or be made to undergo an evil, which he does not deserve. That is, perhaps, the clearest and most emphatic form in which the idea of justice is conceived by the general mind. As it involves the notion of desert, the question arises, what constitutes

desert? Speaking in a general way, a person is understood to deserve good if he does right, evil if he does wrong; and in a more particular sense, to deserve good from those to whom he does or has done good, and evil from those to whom he does or has done evil.

(Mill, 1863/1969, p.153)

Mill (1863/1969, p.169) went on to state that: 'The principle ... of giving to each what they deserve, that is good for good as well as evil for evil, is not only included within the idea of Justice as we have defined it, but is a proper object of that intensity of sentiment.'[1]

A concern for desert appears to have some deep psychological basis to it and is, I think, heavily associated with the reciprocal instinct. Deliberations on what justice entails did not give rise to a concern for desert, but rather an evolved sense of rewarding and punishing based on some conception of desert necessarily informed discussions on justice. Indeed, some desert-driven behaviours may even transcend our own species. For example, the primatologist Frans de Waal has conducted numerous experiments intended to test whether capuchin monkeys demonstrate prosocial tendencies. In one experiment, de Waal (2010) placed two monkeys in a cage that separated them with a wire mesh. Both monkeys were required to pull on a counterweighted tray in order for only one of them to reach a cup of apple slices. It was reported that the monkey that could reach the apple slices would push more of it through the wire mesh to its assistant than when it had to secure the apple slices entirely via its own efforts, and if the assistant was not rewarded as such it was less likely to cooperate in a repeat task.[2] One could interpret these reciprocal rewards and punishments as being motivated by a basic – almost instinctive – sense of desert.

With respect to our own species, the traditional view within the field of child development psychology is that children start to relate earnings to work contributions at about six years of age, but over the last decade evidence has emerged that infants do this from as young as three years, suggesting that it is almost natural for us to be driven to some degree by notions of desert. For example, the psychologists Patricia Kanngiesser and Felix Warneken (2012) reported a study in which thirty-six three- and five-year-olds (eighteen of each) played a fishing game. Each child was paired with a puppet partner and both "fished" for coins, which could be later exchanged for stickers. Importantly, the relative number of coins collected by each partner in a pair could be manipulated by the experimenter by "speeding up" or "slowing down" the puppet. The children, on receiving their sticker rewards, were able to share some of them with their puppet partner. Kanngiesser and Warneken observed that the children, on average, kept significantly more stickers for themselves when they had collected more coins than the puppet than when they had collected fewer, although it is noteworthy that very few children gave the puppet more than half of the total number of stickers available, even when the latter had collected the most coins. A degree of selfish behaviour was thus observed in this study, and the ability to reward according to merit to the extent that the final outcome is definitively disadvantageous to those in control of rewards probably does not develop until middle childhood, but the rudiments of a concern for desert-based rewards appeared to be evident.

A second example is from a study undertaken by the psychologists Katharina Hamann, Johanna Bender and Michael Tomasello (2013), who engaged thirty-two pairs of three-year-olds in a cooperative task. Specifically, the children were required to pull on ropes in order to release and collect marbles, which could then be used to operate a larger toy. For one child in each pair, the rope was not immediately accessible, and they had to perform an additional task in order to reach the rope; i.e. overall, that child was required to do more work than their partner. On pulling the ropes, one child in each pair received three marbles and the other received one marble, with the child who had to do more work sometimes receiving the larger number and sometimes the fewer number of marbles. Bender *et al.* reported that, on average, the children who received three marbles shared more of their "earnings" with their partner when the latter had been required to undertake the additional task to gain access to the rope than when they had not (0.95 marbles versus 0.48 marbles on average) – i.e. when the less fortunate child in terms of marble earnings appeared to be more deserving.[3] The evidence uncovered from economic games suggests that this intrinsic desire to reward on the basis of merit is reinforced in adulthood.

A CONTINUING TASTE FOR DESERT

Let us briefly consider the ultimatum and dictator games, both of which have been tested extensively in the behavioural economics literature, albeit typically in the context of windfall endowments, the receipt of which are relatively unusual in the "real" world. In the ultimatum game, there are two players – Player I and Player II. Player I is given an amount of money (which can be any amount, but assume here it is £10) and is asked to offer a part of it (say, £x) to Player II, who then accepts or rejects the offer. If Player II accepts, he receives £x and Player I is left with £(10−x), but if Player II rejects the offer, both players get nothing. Traditional game theory implies that Player I will want to keep as much money as possible, and for Player II, anything is better than nothing. Thus, the standard rational choice theory prediction is that Player I will offer next to nothing.

The dictator game likewise involves two players, also with an amount of money (let us again assume £10) that Player I is asked to divide. This time, however, Player I does not offer but allocates a share to Player II – Player II has no power to reject the allocation. Player II thus receives £x, Player I is left with £(10−x), and that is the end of the game. Standard rational choice theory predicts that Player I will give Player II nothing.

The predictions of rational choice do not stand up very well in either of these games. Specifically, in the ultimatum game, across many studies, mean offers from those who assume the position of Player I tend to exceed 40 per cent of their endowment, modal offers hover at around 50 per cent and offers less than 20 per cent, though rare, are rejected about half of the time by those who take on the role of Player II.[4] It was thought that the high offers in the ultimatum game might be caused by either strategic play from the proposers (i.e. those placed in the position of Player I) – who, recognising that they may be punished for making low offers, raise them to the point where they think they will just be accepted, thus maximising their expected earnings – or by the proposers possessing a genuine concern for fairness in the distribution of final outcomes. The dictator game, in eliminating the motivation for a strategic response, was designed to test whether the fairness explanation could be unambiguously confirmed. Generally, the mean allocations in the dictator game tend to be somewhat lower than the offers made in the ultimatum game, but are still generally 20–30 per cent of the endowment, albeit with the modal allocation now at 0–20 per cent and with around 20–30 per cent of allocators typically offering nothing.[5] From this we can conclude that although the threat of punishment in the ultimatum game does appear to cause some strategic self-interested behaviours that might falsely be confused as altruistic, applications of the dictator game produce results that imply that substantial residual considerations for fairness in final outcomes remain.

As alluded to above, the endowments of those who assume the position of Player I in the ultimatum and dictator games are typically given and not earned (i.e. they are windfall endowments). This presents an important challenge to the external validity of much of the evidence. One might hypothesise that if the players undertake a task to earn their endowments, then property rights could substantively influence social preferences. The economist Bradley Ruffle (1998) reported a rare example where earned rather than windfall endowments were used in the ultimatum game, albeit with the earnings generated by the responders (rather than the proposers) via their performance on a general knowledge test. Those who performed well and those who performed poorly in the test created endowments of $10 and $4, respectively. The responders' earning ability was reflected in the proportion of the endowment that was offered by the proposers, suggesting that the proposers, on average, felt that those who earned more deserved to be treated better than those who had earned less.[6]

Compared to the ultimatum game, there is more evidence on the impact of earned versus windfall endowments in the dictator game, which points to the important influence that perceptions of desert have on decision-making. The economists Todd Cherry, Peter Frykblom and Jason Shogren (2002), for example, reported a version of the dictator game where allocators first determined the size of the endowment by answering a number of quiz questions, a task similar to that employed by Ruffle (1998). The allocators who performed well and those who performed poorly on the quiz earned endowments of $40 and $10, respectively. Cherry *et al.* reported that, depending on how well they performed on the test, 95–97 per cent of the allocators complied with the rational choice theory prediction of giving nothing to Player II; thus, compared to windfall endowments, other-regarding behaviour was greatly reduced over earned income.

The economists Fredrik Carlsson, Haoran He and Peter Martinsson (2013) aimed to examine the impact of earned money on dictator game responses in a more naturalistic setting. In a university supermarket shop, participants were approached to earn money (50 yuan, about £5 or $7) by completing a survey on the use of supermarket bags. As a control, a separate group of participants were told that they had won windfall money as part of a "Thank You Customer" campaign. To mirror the dictator game largely if not completely, the individuals in both groups were asked if they would be willing to give some of their endowment not to another player, but to charity. The mean offer from the earnings group was 19 per cent of the endowment, compared to 37 per cent in the windfall group. The authors replicated the study in a laboratory setting and reported mean offers of 29 per cent and 74 per cent, respectively, which again suggests that when people earn their endowments they feel as though they are more deserving of it and thus give less of it away.

In addition to testing the effect on allocations when those who assumed the role of Player I had earned the initial endowments in the dictator game, the economists Robert Oxoby and John Spraggon (2008) aimed to observe the effect on Player I responses when those who assumed the role of Player II had earned the endowments. The authors required their participants to earn endowments ranging from $10 to $40, the specific amount of which depended on the number of correct answers to twenty questions in a graduate admissions test. Compared to their control of a mean of 20 per cent of the endowments being allocated in a standard version of the dictator game, Oxoby and Spraggon observed that mean offers were zero when the allocators earned the endowment and exceeded 50 per cent when the recipients were the earners (at least in those cases where the recipients had performed well on the graduate admission test questions; where recipients had performed poorly, offers were similar to those in the control condition). Oxoby and Spraggon concluded that their participants' answers demonstrated that perceived desert dominated any consideration of equality in outcomes.[7]

It is therefore likely that people are driven intrinsically to reward (and punish) people according to whether they perceive those people to be deserving. Most readers, I would surmise, are familiar with how galling it is when they feel that they have not received the credit that they believe they deserve for a particular action (or actions), and have experience of a sense of injustice when they observe that others have been unduly overlooked. However, in terms of using this knowledge as an input into the design of public institutions and interventions it may help to delve a little deeper in relation to exactly when and how much people ought to be credited or blamed for their actions and circumstances.

IDENTIFYING DESERT

Reciprocity, in most circumstances, is unlikely to be sustained in a manner that is healthy and beneficial to all involved parties unless there is, among those concerned, a perceived balance to the exchange, which is where desert often enters. If you were to give someone an expensive bottle of wine for his birthday and he later gifts you a plastic fish slice for yours, then assuming that the other person is not substantially poorer than yourself, future birthday presents are either likely to return to approximate parity with respect to the value of the presents (i.e. you might buy him a spatula next year), or the exchange will fizzle out altogether. Or to give a more extreme example, in modern societies presumably nearly everyone would be appalled if the punishment for stealing a loaf of bread were to have one's hands cut off, because the perpetrator did not deserve that level of punishment for the crime committed.

Although people seem to have some almost instinctive sense of desert, the *extent* to which people are perceived to be deserving of something is often an amorphous concept that may differ interpersonally, as well as across time and place (as the above example of having one's hands chopped off for stealing might indicate). Even if we limit ourselves to perhaps the simplest form of reciprocity bar the instinctive attitudinal type that is common in the animal kingdom (e.g. cats licking each other) – i.e. direct positive dyadic reciprocity – desert can be a malleable, complex concept. For instance, do we prioritise our attention, and/or give most to, those who have given most to us in absolute terms, to those who have given the most relative to their own resources, to those who we know will be quick to put a halt to their reciprocating behaviour if they feel they have been slighted, to those who give the most to others quite apart from ourselves, etc.? Deliberation on the extent to which people are deserving may encompass all of these considerations and more, but they are unified in helping us to identify, engender and sustain the most mutually beneficial long-term reciprocal relationships. Give too much, and you risk breeding resentment (possibly in you and in the recipient) and enforced obligation rather than a free and fair exchange, which would not bode well for long-term (or even short-term) cooperation; give too little and the hope of a long-term reciprocal mutually beneficial relationship will likely be a non-starter.

As already made clear with respect to stealing bread, the argument that people should get only what they deserve extends to the domain of negative reciprocity, to the maxim that the punishment should fit the crime. If the punishment is felt to exceed the crime or vice versa, there will be a prevailing sense that justice has not been served, which may lead to resentment, further retribution, spiralling retaliation and/or a general unwillingness to engage freely in social cooperation.[8] In short, negative reciprocity, which serves to bind groups together by deterring those who might otherwise transgress social norms, will threaten to tear groups apart if desert as a concept is not embraced, explained and widely accepted in the shape of policies, institutions and interventions.[9]

When considering desert in relation to punishment, it is important to recognise that people often act not entirely through volition but due to necessity.[10] For instance, as noted in Chapter 1, when people face extreme scarcity and are in great need, they may face little choice than to act egoistically if they are to survive. Consequently, our response to a person who steals a loaf of bread, for example, is likely to differ if that person is starving than if he is not. Thus, we ought to distinguish between defeasible actions over which a perpetrator is morally responsible and can therefore be blamed fully, and indefeasible actions to which it is harder to attach blame. As Feinberg (1970, p.117) notes:

> [G]eneral rules must list all crimes in the order of their moral
> gravity, all punishments in the order of their severity, and the
> matchings between the two scales. But the moral gravity scale
> would have to list as well motives and purposes, not simply types of
> overt acts, for a given crime can be committed in any kind of
> "mental state," and its "moral gravity" in a given case surely must
> depend in part on its accompanying motive.[11]

In order to judge the defeasibility of an action, one should also distinguish between those that are causal and those that are attributive. That is, in order to fully assign blame for an unwanted outcome, it is insufficient to proclaim that an action caused a harm; one also must attribute an objectionable aspect of the action directly to the harm that has occurred. Feinberg (1970, pp.196–197) relates attributive actions to what he calls triconditional analysis, which consists of: i) the fault condition; ii) the causal condition – i.e. that the act was a cause of the harm; and iii) the causal relevance condition – that the faulty aspect of the act was its causal link to the harm. According to Feinberg, the causal relevance condition goes a long way towards discerning whether someone's action is fully blameworthy (or praiseworthy, if we are in the domain of positive actions).

Feinberg (1970, pp.207–208) presents the following lively scenario to illustrate his argument:

> Consider ... the case of the calamitous soup-spilling at Lady Mary's dinner party. Sir John Stuffgut so liked his first and second bowls of soup that he demanded a third just as Lady Mary was prepared to announce with pride to the hungry and restless guests the arrival of the next course. Sir John's tone was so gruff and peremptory that Lady Mary quite lost her composure. She lifted the heavy tureen with shaking arms and, in attempting to pass it to her intemperate guest, spilled it unceremoniously in the lap of the Reverend Mr. Straightlace.

In this example, one might contend that the causal relevance condition suggests that Sir John's gruffness unsettled Lady Mary, which consequently caused the accident. Sir John is thus to some extent to blame for soiling the reverend's trousers. If Sir John had instead politely requested more soup, although we might still judge him somewhat at fault for his gluttony, the absence of any gruffness to his tone would mean that we would be less inclined to blame him for the soup spillage. As Feinberg (1970, p. 222) notes, 'if the harmful outcome was truly "his fault", the requisite causal connection must have been directly between the faulty aspect of his conduct and the outcome. It is not sufficient to have caused harm *and* to have been at fault if the fault was irrelevant to the causing.'

However, although Sir John's gruffness may have caused the soup to spill, he did not intend for that outcome to occur. Intending

Table 6.1 *A taxonomy of blameworthy actions*

Action type A: An action intended to cause harm and causes that harm.

Action type B: An action intended to cause harm and does not cause that harm.

Action type C: An action unintended to cause harm and causes that harm.
    Action type C_1: The action is objectionable.
    Action type C_2: The action is unobjectionable.

Action type D: An action unintended to cause harm and does not cause that harm.
    Action type D_1: The action is objectionable.
    Action type D_2: The action is unobjectionable.

---

the bad outcome to occur is thus not a prerequisite for some (deserved) degree of blame, but intending as such may scale up the blame that the perpetrator merits. The notion of intention thus allows us to construct the following taxonomy of the degree to which blame is merited for an action that often – but not always – leads to a harmful outcome.

In Table 6.1, Action type A, where a person intends to cause harm and the harm occurs, is the most blameworthy. For example, if Sir John, displeased with Lady Mary's reaction to his request and with the Reverend Mr Straightlace's sanctity, had deliberately pushed the tureen from her hands and into the latter's lap, there can be little doubt that we ought to hold him to account. Action type B occurs when there is a similar intention to harm, but for whatever reason, the intended harm does not occur. For example, Sir John attempts to deliberately push the tureen in the direction of the Reverend Mr Straightlace, but stumbles, falls back into his chair and no soup is spilled. Sir John's intentions are still blameworthy, but since no damage occurred, Action type B is not as blameworthy as Action type A.

Action type C – unintended harm-causing actions – can be broken down into two subtypes, C_1 and C_2, and is reflected in Feinberg's Sir John scenario, summarised above. Sir John did not intend to spill the soup, but in the original scenario his gruffness flustered Lady Mary, which may have contributed to her dropping the tureen. His gruff behaviour was otherwise objectionable – Action type C_1 – and he is thus blameworthy to a degree. If he had politely asked for more soup, we have an example of Action type C_2: his demeanour was otherwise unobjectionable and he did not intend for the soup to be spilled, but his requesting (possibly too much) soup did contribute to the tureen being dropped, and thus he is perhaps still somewhat blameworthy, but not as blameworthy as in Action type C_1.[12] Whether Action type B is more blameworthy than Action type C or vice versa depends upon the trade-off one makes between intentions and outcomes (i.e. B has worse intentions and C has worse outcomes). On a population level this is likely to be an empirical question, but for me, in terms of assigning blame, an intention to harm (even if the harm is not realised) is worse than a non-intentional realised harm (readers may legitimately differ in their view on this).

Finally, Action type D, where there is no intention to cause a harm that is not in any case realised, is of course not blameworthy at all, but this too can be broken down into two subtypes, D_1 and D_2, where in the former the person's behaviour is otherwise objectionable and in the latter it is not. In terms of Sir John and the tureen, D_1 and D_2 are identical to C_1 and C_2 with the important exception that the soup is not in fact spilled. The only reason for differentiating between D_1 and D_2 here is not to apportion blame, but to recognise that those who commit Action type D_1 (compared to D_2) are more likely to meet Feinberg's fault condition if a relevant harm was to occur in the future (and also one might want to avoid inviting such people to dinner parties).

This attempt at identifying different levels of deserved blame informs the debate on what might be the correct application of negative reciprocity, and, as noted, extends in its mirror image to the identification of deserved credit in informing positive reciprocity. For instance, an intention to benefit someone that is realised as an outcome would surely deserve some consideration of a return in kind.

I will leave it to the reader to work through all of the permutations of Table 6.1 in the positive domain, but it is clear that when it comes to considering the notion of desert – i.e. when it comes to deciding with whom to reciprocate (and by how much) – intentions and outcomes both matter to many of us.[13] Although it might not always be easy to discern intentions nor link intentions directly to outcomes, this discussion is thus relevant when considering what might be a proportionate response to others' actions in both the private sphere of people's lives and for informing the design of public policy.

Thus, in thinking about the notion of desert, a person's intended actions and consequent outcomes towards others both matter. But might there be occasions when their intentions and consequent outcomes towards themselves matter too?

THE DESERVING POOR

In the most influential theory in political philosophy since the Second World War, John Rawls (1999) argued that if each of us was unaware of our position in the world (i.e. if we were placed behind his famous veil of ignorance), then out of self-interest we would choose to focus our attention on improving the situation of those who are the worst off, because for all we know, we could be among them. The argument is that a proper consideration of justice would preclude the consideration of our own positions, tastes and life experiences when making a judgement on how society ought to be organised; that the scenario focuses our minds on how we would wish to be treated by others, and leads us to treat others in that same way. Thus, justice, in this theory, equates to maximising the minimum: maximin.[14]

However, we do not live in a transcendental world, and the success and sustainability of policy interventions and institutions depend upon how people react to them in reality. For that, we must consider people's perceptions of how to organise society when their own positions, tastes and life experiences are known to them – i.e. when the veil of ignorance is lifted. It is of course possible – even likely – that many would still opt for a maximin policy direction (or at least for a direction that helps the worst off to some degree), for a host of reasons, including the reputational benefits that may be garnered from signalling as such and even pure altruism, but many others might demand an indication that those at the bottom *deserve* any assistance that is directed towards them.[15]

As noted by Feinberg (1970), rewards and punishment may be given in response to gratitude and resentment, and many might feel gratitude towards those who benefit from public programmes if they offered something tangible in return, which could in turn ensure the continued support for and sustainability of those programmes. This takes us back into the realm of the desert-based arguments discussed earlier (i.e. desert in relation to the intentions and outcomes directed at others). For example, a structure could be put in place for people in receipt of welfare to volunteer to undertake some hours of public works each week if they are physically and mentally able, and the total number of voluntary hours committed across a population could be widely disseminated on a weekly or monthly basis. As a form of conditional cash transfer, people in receipt of welfare could of course be *required* to undertake such work for them to continue to receive support, but a non-voluntary requirement might breed resentment. Although the notion of expecting people in receipt of welfare to offer something tangible back to society while they are in receipt of support will be unpalatable to some, a refusal to work if one is able in such circumstances is a form of free riding – or egoism – that can damage the groups of which we are all a part.

However, Feinberg (1970) also contends that rewards/benefits and punishments/costs may be given in recognition that someone has done something good or bad, without any consideration of gratitude or resentment attached. He states, for instance, that: 'When the father paid his son a quarter, he acknowledged his son's achievement without necessarily feeling any joy, gratitude, or any other emotion' (Feinberg, 1970, p.70), and perhaps this argument can be extended to more profound domains where people have done "good" (or not done "bad") to themselves. For instance, if it is perceived that an individual is personally responsible for his misfortune, then many might take the view that he is less deserving of assistance than if his misfortune is beyond his control. This type of scenario is sometimes discussed in relation to the prioritisation of public health care resources; i.e. if someone suffers ill health, can we make a case that he ought to be a greater priority if his misfortune is the result of genetics or accident than if it is the consequence of his own personal lifestyle choices (e.g. see Le Grand, 1991)? There are, however, problems in attributing ill health (or other misfortunes) to personal responsibility, to which I will return in Chapter 8.

Of course, it is unlikely that many of those who adjudge people to be undeserving according to the above criteria would withhold assistance entirely (not least because they recognise that recipients of assistance, as fellow citizens and probable sometime taxpayers, may feel entitled to public sector services), but the emphasis may shift somewhat from desert to charity, from reciprocity to pure altruism. Feinberg (1970, pp.75–76) makes the same point when he writes:

> When a person suffers a loss, it may be the fault of another person or it may be no one's fault ... the nature of desert differs in the two cases. There is, however, a third possibility: the loss or injury may be his own fault. In that case, though he may well be entitled to help, we should be loath to say that he deserved it; for we do not as a rule compensate people for their folly or indolence, and even when we do, it is not because we think they deserve it. Herein lies the difference between helping a person out of a jam simply through charitable beneficence and giving him aid he deserves .... There is nothing pitiable about a person who deserves help.

Feinberg thus suggests that there is something pitiable about a person who is in receipt of charity. If welfare and other forms of publicly provided benefits are generally perceived as charity – as pity-driven acts of pure altruism – rather than as being deserved, this may have implications with respect to the size and sustainability of the assistance given. Feinberg (1970, p.87) contended that 'desert is a *moral* concept in the sense that it is logically prior to and independent of public institutions and their rules, not in the sense that it is an instrument of an ethereal "moral" counterpart of our public institutions', and earlier in this chapter I presented evidence that suggests that people, probably from a very young age, are indeed driven by notions of desert. If one wants to secure the best chance that substantive welfare programmes will exist into the future, it is a matter of sensible strategy to design them so that it is clear that the people whom they benefit are seen as deserving.

I have reviewed three notions of desert in this chapter, at least two of which are associated with different degrees of desert that depend upon people's intentions and the consequent outcomes. Those are that people: (i) deserve something positive for intending/causing something good for others; (ii) deserve something negative for intending/causing something bad for others; and (iii) deserve something positive for intending/causing something good (or preventing something bad) for themselves. Desert, and the associated concept of reciprocity, are stronger human motivational forces than pure altruism, and the strength and sustainability of public sector services and welfare systems (not to mention our private relationships and collaborations) may rely on a broad acceptance of this argument.

FOOD FOR THOUGHT

1. Other than desert, what might legitimately inform justice?
2. Is an intended yet unmaterialised harm more blameworthy than an unintentional harm?
3. Should recipients of welfare be expected to undertake public works?

7   Private Matters

In Chapter 6 it was asserted that considerations of desert are important to how humans react to each other – to how they reward, benefit, chastise and punish one another – and thus that it is a useful notion in relation to how public policy might be designed, and how private decisions can be understood. I argued that considerations of desert lie deep within the human breast, a view expressed by the psychologists Christina Starmans, Mark Sheskin and Paul Bloom (2017, p.4), who wrote that:

> To treat everyone equally would entail penalization of more
> productive individuals when they collaborate with less productive
> individuals relative to highly productive individuals. In contrast
> with equality, fairness allows individuals with different levels
> of productivity to share the benefits of their collaboration
> proportionately. This focus on fairness is particularly important for
> humans (compared with even our closest evolutionary relatives),
> due to the critical importance of collaboration in human hunting
> and foraging.[1]

However, although desert-based reciprocity is important, it is not, of course, the only legitimate consideration, and its relative importance, like almost everything in behavioural public policy, is likely to be to some extent contextual.

For example, as also noted in the previous chapter with respect to Rawlsian theory, there are good arguments in favour of inequality in incomes beyond what might reasonably be contended are a consequence of desert, in that it may serve as a driver of aspiration and generate economic growth. If this holds true, then the incentive of financial gain could make possible the creation of so much wealth in the aggregate that even the shares directed to the relatively disadvantaged may be greater than the equally shared slices of a smaller equalitarian pie. On the flip side, there are legitimate arguments against even merit-aligned inequality in opportunities and incomes in order to create a more representative distribution of, for example, different ethnicities and genders in particular positions, and/or to protect social cohesion and trust. Moreover, many people are likely to be supportive of efforts to alleviate to some extent the needs and burdens of those who, strictly speaking, have done little to *deserve* assistance. People may also sometimes be reluctant to reciprocate with others, even if those others merit such consideration, if the consequence of such action would be to widen the inequality between the two parties.[2]

There will therefore be those who call for less equality than merit-based desert prescribes, and others who want more equality than it would allow. The same person might wish for more or less equality than desert prescribes *depending* on the circumstances, whereas other people will want more or less equality irrespective of desert, *whatever* the circumstances. However, it remains the contention here that for most people, much of the time, desert is an important, albeit often implicit, consideration in informing their personal interactions and in how they think public policy and welfare programmes ought to be designed.

The discussion in this chapter is limited to a consideration of the extent to which governments should attempt to influence people's personal lifestyle choices and behaviours; i.e. those that are generally believed to lie beyond the scope of what are, in many countries, accepted public sector policy objectives, such as health from health care, literacy and numeracy from education, poverty alleviation from income support programmes, etc.[3] As will be clear from earlier chapters in this book, I will contend that with respect to private actions that impose no substantive externalities on others, government intervention, beyond an educative function and a very general shaping of the environment so as to sustain people's natural inclination towards engaging in mutually beneficial actions, ought to be limited to the point of being non-existent. Certainly, in these circumstances, governments, I will argue, should neither manipulate nor coerce, no matter how well intentioned their motives might be.

CURTAILING INTERFERENCE

Within the liberal tradition there will be instances where a strong argument can be made that it is justifiable for governments to manipulate and/or coerce people with respect to their personal lifestyle choices and behaviours. A stark example is the lockdown of citizens, businesses and educational activities in response to the global coronavirus pandemic. In such circumstances, however, it is my contention that the principal justification for such invasive interventions is centred on externality considerations (which includes the pressure that the infected place on health care systems), in this case in relation to an infectious and potentially highly harmful virus against which there was, for almost a year, no protective vaccine. The liberal tradition does not allow a purely paternalistic justification for such severe infractions on individual liberty. Attempts to educate people about the virus and the potential related consequences of their behaviours are of course supported under liberalism, but there would be no attempt to manipulate or coerce people in any particular direction unless mitigating externalities is the objective.[4]

To revisit and combine some of the material presented in Chapters 2 and 3, behavioural welfare economists and libertarian paternalists contend that people are not at fault for the behavioural affects that lead them to act, behave and decide against their own best interests (as deliberatively judged by themselves), and that they thus deserve to be given a guiding hand in order for them to improve their decision-making. Let us take the example of the man, introduced in note 3, who eats five doughnuts every day. A libertarian paternalist may argue that due to present bias, this man is automatically overweighing present enjoyments at the expense of possible long-term deleterious consequences to his health – consequences that if he were to reflect upon deliberatively may in fact, for him, outweigh the present enjoyments. That is, through no fault of his own, present bias is causing him to make decisions that his "rational" self might reject. The libertarian paternalist would thus contend that it is legitimate for governments (or others) to manipulate the man's automatic response mode such that he is more likely to make decisions in the moment that align with what he would choose to do following a period of reflection, and a way to do this is to alter in some way the context in which the man makes his doughnut consumption choices. For example, next to his favourite doughnut counter, the government might recommend the placement of a "before and after" caricature, with the "before" segment depicting a healthy-looking individual with a slim body, clear skin and a fine set of teeth, and the "after" segment depicting a less presentable likeness than that given "before". The underlying intention of this intervention would be to try to make the potential future more present to doughnut eaters, motivating some of them to voluntarily moderate their consumption to match their deliberative view of what is in their own interests. This would be a classic nudge at the point of purchase.

Those who adopt the liberal perspective would counter that we should attempt to educate people as to the future potential consequences of eating too many doughnuts if we have good information on the matter, but ultimately, so long as the doughnut eater is not harming anyone else, the number of doughnuts that he consumes is nobody's business but his own. To reiterate an argument made by Sugden (2009), it might not even be possible to uncover a person's deliberative preferences; an attempt to do so may well reveal a less accurate picture of what a person wants to do with his life than his less reflective choices suggest. In short, the best indicator of what a person wants to do may well be what he does. Consequently, liberalism stands against attempts at manipulating people viscerally at the point of consumption if externalities are not a relevant consideration – i.e. if the intervention is purely an instrument of paternalism.

However, if it can be demonstrated that the person's doughnut-eating patterns are genuinely likely to harm others then we have a legitimate justification for regulating against their excessive consumption. This does not mean that the government would *necessarily* choose to regulate in such circumstances. One could make the argument, hopefully with supporting evidence, that a person who consumes five doughnuts each day is, as a direct consequence, likely to place a heavier strain on health care services than would have otherwise been the case, and if he lives in a country with a publicly financed health care system, others will have to cross-subsidise his health care treatment (assuming that those who cause their own health problems remain eligible for public sector health care), a clear externality argument. However, since those who consume an excessive number of doughnuts are likely to be quite a small proportion of the total population, since it is difficult to monitor doughnut consumption patterns, and since the direct link between eating doughnuts and requiring health care treatment will perhaps always be nebulous, regulation (or manipulation) intended to limit the number of doughnuts that a person consumes each day would be too much of an intrusion into personal lifestyle choices from a liberal perspective.[5]

To reiterate, the political economy of behavioural public policy that I am proposing is consistent with the classical liberal framework: specifically, if people are not unduly harming others, they should be free of manipulative and coercive government intervention. If liberty is respected as such, some people will desire to compete with others to provide a particular good or service as an outlet for an entrepreneurial urge that would help them to achieve their own conception of a flourishing life. Yet it is sometimes said that although competition can bring out the best in people it can also bring out the worst; that it has an indisputable capacity to cause harms. Knowing this, should people be allowed to compete with each other in the provision of private goods and services?

A COMPETITIVE EDGE

There are two principal domains that are relevant to human actions, behaviours and decisions: those pertaining to social interactions (e.g. family, friends) and those pertaining to economic exchange (e.g. purchasing, work).[6] Some scholars have argued that there is a qualitative difference in the motivational drivers underpinning these domains.[7] For example, the social anthropologist Marcel Mauss (1954) believed that exchange driven by the law of economic interest via money transactions is inferior to the gift exchange (i.e. the binding social exchanges that are common in hunter-gatherer societies), because the latter, infused with mutual obligations and dependent upon trust, is better than an appeal to the egoistic self-interest that he argued was a characteristic of the former. The social policy analyst Richard Titmuss (1970/1997) agreed with Mauss, and maintained that social policy, unlike economic policy, focuses more on institutions that create integration and discourage alienation, although here Titmuss was stepping into the realm of public policy rather than private social actions. A little earlier, the sociologist Peter Blau (1964) had argued that the difference between a social exchange and an economic exchange is that in the former, although a return is expected, it is usually a future obligation that is not precisely specified, and the nature of what is exchanged is left to the discretion of the giver. However, Blau's fellow sociologist Anthony Heath (1976) remarked that social exchanges are much more formalised than Blau suggests, with, for example, the division of labour in the family often prescribed. Heath thus implied that the distinction between economic and social exchange may be one of degree (e.g. in the balance between obligation and self-interest), rather than there being a qualitative difference. The contention in this book is that considerations of mutuality can substantively impact upon economic and social exchanges in the private sphere of people's lives, but that in both the actions of at least some people will be fuelled by egoism. In this section I will limit myself to a discussion of whether there is a case for government intervention to disallow competition in the domain in which people make their private economic exchanges.

Followers of the liberal tradition believe that the competitive market is the best means by which to secure social cooperation, which will in turn serve to produce efficient market exchange. This sentiment can be illustrated using Smith's (1776/1999) classic rendering of the butcher, the baker and the brewer. Although Smith maintained that none of these tradespersons relies on gratitude and a mutuality of interests in order for there to be among them an optimal exchange of goods, if one party were to attempt to exploit the other the trading relationship among them would collapse since the exploited party would seek out an alternative exchange partner.[8] As suggested by Anderson (2017), in implicitly assuming that everyone is self-employed, Smith did not sufficiently foresee the appalling working conditions and below-subsistence remuneration to which large segments of the wage labour class were exposed during the nineteenth century and beyond, who were squeezed by employers responding to the harmful incentives that are often embedded in the competitive market. Due to a lack of "voice" – i.e. a lack of authority and agency – for the majority of wage earners, far from being a mechanism for fair reciprocal exchange, Anderson contends that the competitive market has been an instrument that has caused suffering for millions of people.

It is also perhaps worth reminding ourselves that Smith's exposition with respect to these three types of artisan focused upon simple goods. One might conclude that there is not a huge potential for market failures – particularly asymmetries of information between the buyer and seller – in the trade for meat, bread and beer.[9] That is, the buyer of meat (or bread or beer) may quickly become as adept as the seller at assessing the quality of the product, and if the buyer is not happy, then, as noted above, in a competitive market he can go elsewhere. In the words of Friedman and Friedman (1980/1990, p.226): 'The consumer is protected from being exploited by one seller by the existence of another seller from whom he can buy and who is eager to sell to him.' Yet when the product or service under consideration is more complex than meat, bread and beer, there may be significant asymmetries of information between the buyer and the seller (or between different sellers), and thus considerable potential for the latter to exploit the former.[10]

As argued in Chapter 3, although supporting the notion of competition, many of the most prominent liberal economists did not condone an attitude of unhindered laissez-faire with respect to the workings of the economy, which is worth emphasising given that such ideas are often attributed to them under the misleading label of neoliberalism. For example, Hayek (1944/2001, p.37) wrote that:

> It is important not to confuse opposition to ... planning with a dogmatic laissez-faire attitude. The liberal argument is in favour of making the best possible use of the forces of competition as a means of co-ordinating human efforts, not an argument for leaving things just as they are. It is based on the conviction that where effective competition can be created, it is a better way of guiding individual efforts than any other. It does not deny, but even emphasises, that, in order that competition should work beneficially, a carefully thought-out legal framework is required .... Nor does it deny that where it is impossible to create the conditions necessary to make competition effective, we must resort to other methods of guiding economic activity.

Moreover, Hayek (1944/2001, p.125) recognised that there are circumstances where many people cannot make adequate provisions for themselves via a private market – for example, for comprehensive health care insurance, and for assistance in the event of a natural disaster. Hayek maintained that the case for the state to provide insurance for these eventualities is strong and does not undermine freedom, but it is clear that he believed that a private competitive market should be used whenever and wherever it can be made to work.[11]

A strong element of desert is embedded in a perfect market (i.e. buyers get what they pay for, and suppliers are remunerated fairly for what they sell). Moreover, a major benefit of the competitive market according to, for instance, Hayek (1944/2001) and Friedman and Friedman (1980/1990), is that it is the only economic system designed to minimise the power exercised by man over man. Perhaps that is true, but while not condoning laissez-faire, while admonishing egoistic tendencies, and while placing great faith in the competitive market as a means of forging social cooperation, it ought to be admitted that many liberal scholars may have underestimated the degree to which, via informational asymmetries and the behavioural influences, some partners to an exchange can work to exploit others. As indicated earlier in this book, Mill did not himself acknowledge explicitly that an individual or organisation would use what we now label as loss aversion, present bias and the like to undermine a free and fair exchange, but such interference, together with the exploitation of informational advantage, may be used covertly to impose harms on people by manipulating their choices and actions in directions that they would otherwise not choose to go. Government attempts to mitigate interferences of this kind therefore appear allowable under Mill's harm principle (Mill, 1859/1969). Some may contend that the competitive market can render mute the exploitative potential of information asymmetries and the behavioural influences, with the argument being that, over the medium to long term, suppliers that use these tactics will be "found out" by consumers, who will then drive them from the market. However, these challenges to a free and fair exchange may often be somewhat stickier than this narrative suggests, particularly with respect to irregular purchases (e.g. cars, houses), and in their book *Phishing for Phools* the economists George Akerlof and Robert Shiller (2015) reveal that in certain sectors these attempts at exploitation – which are a part of what Sunstein (2020) and others have labelled "sludge" – have for a long time been rife.[12]

My arguments in this book depart a little from those of the classical liberals – in particular, from the Austrian School – in that I emphasise somewhat more forcefully the potential harms of the competitive market. I contend that long-term mutuality of interests and social cooperation, particularly over goods and services that are associated with substantial asymmetries of information and the behavioural influences, cannot be assumed to be an inevitability in a competitive market; rather, those types of relationships have to be consciously fostered (or, at the very least, protected), even if they ultimately sit well with the almost innate human tendency to recipro-cate. Egoistic temptations are also strong, and will always be acted upon by some, with or without the presence of competition. On balance, the case for offering people alternative sources if they feel that their current supplier is not fulfilling their side of a mutually agreeable exchange (or, indeed, allowing a range of potential suppliers when the buyer is considering purchasing a good or service for the first time), is a difficult proposition to dismiss in the *private* sphere of people's lives, even given the incentives for suppliers to exploit market failures and the behavioural influences to misrepresent the quality of their products. However, in a liberal society, perhaps the most important argument for allowing competition is that people should be free to pursue their own private objectives in life (again assuming that no substantive harms are imposed on others), and for many one of those objectives might be to supply a product or service that others are also supplying.[13] It would be too much of an intrusion into people's lives if there were laws prohibiting them from doing so. Harms are, of course, likely to occur, but as argued by Hayek (1944/ 2001) and many others, governments can try to regulate against the worst excesses of the competitive market.

Given that the competitive market can fuel incentives for people to act egoistically and, by doing so, impose harms, there is, as stated, a clear case for governments to regulate against such actions. But is there a case for government interventions that attempt to crowd out the urge to act egoistically to begin with?

APPEALING TO OUR BETTER ANGELS

Feinberg (1970, p.236) wrote that: 'There is perhaps no better index to solidarity than vicarious pride and shame.' He suggests, I think, that if we feel a sense of pride in what those around us are doing, and a sense of shame with respect to those who transcend the accepted social norms, then this serves as an indication of the strength of the societies in which we live. Feinberg (1970, p.248) went on to argue that: 'No individual person can be blamed for not being a hero or a saint (what a strange "fault" that would be!), but a whole people can be blamed for not producing a hero when the times require it, especially when the failure can be charged to some discernible element in the group's "way of life" that militates against heroism.' These quotations support the notion that people attach an intrinsic positive (or negative) feeling to the way in which the society in which they live is structured, organised and characterised – the values in which the society itself and in general imbues.[14] In other words, individuals will *desire* to live in a particular type of society. Perhaps obviously, there will not be complete consensus on what type of society is preferred; that is, the desired type of society will differ interpersonally. However, it is not unrealistic to assume that most people desire a society that encourages, or at least does not discourage, mutuality of respect and in actions and care for those who are perceived to be deserving of assistance over one that crowds in avarice and egoism.

Some of the ways in which governments can nourish reciprocal motivations were introduced in Chapter 5 and include emphasising its importance in the political and policy rhetoric, tackling excessive income and wealth concentrations, and decentralising governance structures. At least some of these measures, if enacted, will of course impact upon public as well as private decision-making, but if we limit the argument here to the private sphere of our lives, the contention is that reciprocal actions can help us to achieve our personal goals, whatever our desires (which may or may not include some conception of utility) might be.

There are of course many different forms of interaction between various actors in society, but in keeping with the economic domain of our private lives, a major exchange relationship is that between the employer and the employee. Contrasting somewhat with Anderson's (2017) concern that wage labour is often unjustly squeezed in a competitive market, Akerlof (1982) argued that a higher than necessary wage is often offered by employers in the expectation that employees will reciprocate by working harder than egoistic self-interest dictates, a conjecture for which there is experimental support (some of which I summarised in my *Reciprocity* book).[15] One potential role for government is therefore to educate employers that remuneration, or even just a general disposition, towards their workforce that they might otherwise perceive as unduly generous might well foster a more mutually beneficial relationship. Moreover, if this reasoning is correct then those who have contended that a (reasonably generous) minimum wage policy is economically suboptimal might not be accurate in their conjecture, although this may rely on whether employees believe that their employers are paying the minimum wage willingly or under protest.

In addition to paying what is perceived to be a fair wage, a pay-for-performance mechanism in which employees are given small bonuses for achieving particular preset quality criteria, might also be used to take advantage of the natural human drive to reciprocate. Such quality criteria could be used to incentivise particular tasks that might otherwise receive insufficient attention, and the financial incentives may not need to be large in order to be effective. Indeed, if the incentives are perceived as a reminder that certain tasks should not be overlooked rather than as a material inducement, they may not need to involve money at all. They could instead use the almost innate concern that people have for their own reputations (on which more below), and thus comprise, for example, employee-of-the-month awards (which could count towards promotions).[16] The government ought to have no role, of course, in forcing pay-for-performance mechanisms on private employers, but if these instruments are found to work then the government could disseminate knowledge of their potential benefits.

In the other important exchange relationship in the private economy – i.e. that between buyers and sellers – it is often in the interests of both parties to forge long-term reciprocal relationships that are built on trust, particularly for goods and services that buyers purchase reasonably regularly.[17] Hume (1751/2018, pp.81–82) wrote that:

By our own continual and earnest pursuit of a character, a name, a reputation in the world, we bring our own deportment and conduct frequently in review, and consider how they appear in the eyes of those who approach and regard us. This constant habit of surveying ourselves, as it were, in reflection, keeps alive all the sentiments of right and wrong, and begets, in noble natures, a certain reverence for themselves as well as others, which is the surest guardian of every virtue.

As noted above and discussed in depth elsewhere, a concern for one's own and for others' reputations and standing lies deep within the human breast, and can, and does, play a substantive role in attempting to forge and sustain the trust between buyers and sellers that serves their mutual interests (e.g. Oliver, 2019).[18]

Indeed, by signalling whether or not persons we do not know deserve our positive attention, cooperation and/or patronage, reputation is the nutrient of indirect reciprocity. In these circumstances, to inform their decisions buyers substitute others' experiences with sellers for the direct experiences that they lack. The egoistically inclined will always be tempted to obfuscate – to use market failures and the behavioural influences to deceive people with respect to how trustworthy they really are; over quite long periods, particularly if they sell goods or services that people consume irregularly, they might benefit from acting on these instincts. A legitimate role for government in this context might therefore be to discern which suppliers are offering genuinely good-quality services and products, and to attempt to educate citizens not only of their findings, but also on what they based those findings.

A final important exchange relationship in the sphere of private decision-making is that which citizens have with each other. With respect to donating blood, the economist Kenneth Arrow (1972, p.349) noted that many people are driven to act prosocially due to an implicit recognition of mutual interest when he wrote that 'perhaps, one gives good things, such as blood, in exchange for a generalized obligation on the part of fellow men to help in other circumstances if needed'. The Behavioural Insights Team (2013) used this suggestion (or something close to it) when testing how, via messaging, organ donor registration rates might be increased in the United Kingdom. The authors randomly assigned over one million people to receive one of eight messages when renewing their driving licences, with each message framed according to a behavioural influence. They found that the most effective message, which they estimated would lead to an additional 96,000 organ donor registrations each year, was one that was informed by reciprocity.[19] One might conclude that this potential government intervention is manipulative, but a counterargument is that it is merely serving to preserve and reinforce that which most humans find natural (i.e. mutuality). It might thus sit quite close to the call to emphasise the importance of reciprocity in the policy rhetoric. Moreover, the intervention is in any case principally targeting otherwise forgone positive externalities (i.e. a shortage of organs for those who need them), and is thus allowable in a liberal framework.

To conclude this chapter, it will not by now be surprising to state that there is no role for manipulative or coercive government paternalism over the private domain of decision-making in my political economy of behavioural public policy. Followers of the liberal economic tradition contend that the competitive market is the best means by which to foster social cooperation, and over simple goods, and indeed sometimes over complex goods, this may be true. However, we cannot ignore the fact that the competitive market harbours significant incentives for egoism, particularly in the provision of goods and services that are associated with market failures and where there is scope to exploit the behavioural influences. That said, private decisions that impose unacceptable externalities can be regulated against if needs be, and importantly, in the realm of private decision-making, where people ought to be free to pursue their desires (which includes entering competition with others if they so wish), the need to protect autonomy outweighs the arguments to disallow the competitive market entirely. Moreover, the competitive market offers a means to protect people from poor goods and services by there being alternative suppliers. However, governments do have a role to play in protecting and nurturing the reciprocal instincts that have evolved over eons to help us in the pursuit of our own desires and in guiding us to facilitate others to follow theirs. It is apt now to ask whether the same arguments hold up in the public domain of decision-making.

FOOD FOR THOUGHT

1. Is government manipulation to reduce a person's consumption of doughnuts legitimate?
2. Does the competitive market over private decision-making cause more harm than good?
3. Does pure altruism or enlightened self-interest motivate people to donate blood?

8   Public Matters

The writer Edward Bellamy, in his nineteenth-century fantasy novel *Looking Backward*, depicted a preacher attempting to explain how a socialist utopia had emerged in America in the one hundred years since the book's protagonist, Julian West (now awake), fell asleep. The preacher states that:

> It finds its simple and obvious explanation in the reaction of a changed environment upon human nature. It means merely that a form of society which was founded on the pseudo self-interest of selfishness, and appealed solely to the anti-social and brutal side of human nature, has been replaced by institutions based on the true self-interest of a rational unselfishness, and appealing to the social and generous instincts of men.
>
> *(Bellamy, 1888/1996, p.134)*

Bellamy, of course, went too far, and for a number of reasons. For instance, the idea that there could be a socialist utopia in America makes the novel fully deserving of being labelled a fantasy, but also, the very term "socialist utopia" is, I contend, an oxymoron. This is because humans have a deep instinctive desire to be free, and most forms of socialism, particularly when instituted into practice, do not respect autonomy. The authoritarianism that is therefore inevitably embedded in socialism is thus at odds with what most of us desire. Moreover, socialism tends to rely on the notion that people are natural altruists, but most of us are not, at least not in the pure sense of the term, no matter how much we might otherwise protest. We are natural reciprocators: we are liberals, not socialists.

Bellamy himself hints at our almost instinctive liberal tendencies when he refers to 'the true self-interest of rational unselfishness', and suggests, as I have done, that this motivator of human behaviour can be crowded in or crowded out, to replace or to be replaced by selfish short-sighted egoism, depending on how the environment and society that surrounds us is structured and framed.[1] In Chapter 7, I argued that we should aim to nurture the motivation to behave reciprocally over private activities while at the same time fully respect the desire for autonomous actions, so long as the latter do not impose undue harms on others. But what of decisions relating to goods and services (usually services) that a society has decided ought to be delivered by public arrangement?

Public sector services (health care, education, etc.) are services that were once delivered privately if they were delivered at all, and indeed in some countries they are still predominantly a private concern. If a society decides that these services ought to fall within the domain of private decision-making, then I contend that the arguments presented in Chapter 7 apply to them entirely. However, the majority view in most societies evolved over time to coalesce on the notion that there are some services that focus on producing outcomes that are fundamental to people in their pursuit of their own private objectives in life, whatever those objectives might be, and yet it is difficult, perhaps impossible, for these services to be provided efficiently and equitably through private actions.[2] If people are abjectly miserable or ignorant due to circumstances beyond their own control, their capacity to flourish is much diminished. Therefore, it is legitimate for governments to introduce corrective measures (i.e. public sector services) so that people can more fully partake in their own lives. However, relieving misery and ignorance is not the converse of a government-sponsored pursuit of happiness on a pleasure–pain continuum. Rather, it is an attempt to provide, or at least improve, the basic circumstances required for people to be able to follow their desires, in relation to which happiness (or welfare or utility) may well be, at most, only a second-order consideration for many of us.[3]

Although the reader will by now know that I place a large premium on individual autonomy and freedom, enforced collective action is warranted if, without it, the threat to each individual's capacity to flourish is stark. A dramatic example of a circumstance such as this was referred to in Chapter 7; namely, the global corona-virus pandemic. Most governments sooner or later realised that they needed to curtail freedoms temporarily to secure the right circum-stances for longer-term freedoms to flourish (it remains to be seen whether governments will curtail freedoms in response to the climate crisis). However, government intervention to secure public sector services is usually less dramatic than this. As aforementioned, it usually follows, at least in part, from a realisation across society that people need some basic level of some types of good or service – related to, for example, health, education or income – in order for them to have reasonable opportunities to pursue their desires – of flourishing – on their own terms. But if we establish health or education services, for instance, to focus on the production of broadly agreed-upon out-comes (e.g. the production of health, the reduction of health inequal-ities, improved access to hospitals, safe and compassionate care of elderly people, literacy and numeracy standards at particular ages, school examination pass rates, etc.), then within those services some freedoms will necessarily have to be curtailed.[4] The persons providing and using a health care service, for example, will be required to focus principally on the agreed-upon goals, and not on some other objective that they desire from that service. Before considering in a little more detail the aspects of allowable private sphere desires that ought to be limited in the domain of public sector decision-making, it might be instructive to return briefly to some of the classical liberals, and their views on whether government intervention to provide public sector services is at all justifiable.

A LIBERAL COMMON GOAL

Echoing the above, Mill believed that government ought to provide public education because, without it, the uncultivated would prob-ably not be able to discern that they want to be cultivated, and even if they were able to discern as such, they would lack the means and wherewithal to educate themselves.[5] Mill, perhaps rightly, went further than hinting that education facilitates a flourishing life, however; he also maintained that there are positive externalities from a public education system, by it raising the character of individuals, which consequently benefits society. Mill (1848/1970, p.318) stated that: 'Education … is one of those things which it is admissible in principle that a government should provide for the people. The case is one to which the reasons of the non-interference principle do not necessarily or universally extend.'[6]

As noted in Chapter 1, von Mises, a liberal of the Austrian School, disparaged Mill's later-in-life views for being, he thought, socialist, and he disagreed that education ought to be provided by the state.[7] Von Mises (1927/2005, p.xx) wrote that:

> All that social policy can do is to remove the outer causes of pain and suffering; it can further a system that feeds the hungry, clothes the naked, and houses the homeless. Happiness and contentment do not depend on food, clothing, and shelter, but, above all, on what a man cherishes within himself. It is not from a disdain of spiritual goods that liberalism concerns itself exclusively with man's material well-being, but from a conviction that what is highest and deepest in man cannot be touched by any outward regulation. It seeks to produce only outer well-being because it knows that inner-spiritual riches cannot come to man from without, but only from within his own heart. It does not aim at creating anything but the outward preconditions for the development of the inner life.

I personally contend that people wish to fulfil desires (and that some, but not all, people desire only "happiness and contentment"), but von Mises's view remains in line with the notion that the purpose of providing some goods and services publicly via government intervention is to help people who otherwise face severe constraints in the pursuit of their private goals. He simply did not believe that education is a service that should be taken out of the domain of private decision-making to support that objective.[8]

Hayek also of course believed that when it comes to private economic actions, individualism leads to progress, whereas collectivism, with shared goals and processes and no tolerance for divergent views, leads to stagnation. But Hayek recognised that this perspective does not apply to everything; he wrote that: 'We can rely on voluntary agreement to guide the action of the state ... so long as it is confined to spheres where agreement exists' (Hayek, 1944/2001, p.64). Thus, if it is commonly agreed that decent levels of particular functionings – e.g. health, literacy – are necessary for people to satisfy their own desires, then it would appear that Hayek too would support government-sponsored collectivism in the pursuit of these common objectives.

Overall, then, within the liberal tradition there is general support for publicly provided services that produce outcomes that are thought foundational for people to pursue their private desires, although liberal thinkers appear to have different views on which services it is legitimate to deliver publicly for this purpose. Thus, to summarise, although liberals contend that in the private sphere of decision-making the only role for government interference in individual decision-making (if they accept any role at all), beyond the amelioration of harms, is to create the general conditions for people to better pursue their own various and varied goals in life (i.e. their private desires, in my conception of liberalism), public services exist to focus upon the just delivery of collectively agreed-upon objectively defined outcomes, outcomes that can be considered in some sense "primary".

However, some scholars question whether we can really hone in on particular sectors as delivering outcomes that can be identified as primary at all.[9] For instance, in relation to alleviating a poor state of health, Le Grand and New (2015) contend that a severely handicapped person with a desire to travel the world might want money instead of health care. Referencing the UK's National Health Service, they also ask why no one calls for a National Food Service, since nutrition is of fundamental importance to all of us.[10] On the first point, it is perhaps worth highlighting that governments in many countries have income

support programmes, and while this support is unlikely to be sufficient to finance global travel it is, in part, often able to facilitate
people with respect to their private desires, at least to some degree.
Thus, in some countries, a particular level of income is essentially
seen as a primary good, with the income level dependent upon the
country's wealth, cost of living, prevailing values in society, etc.[11]
A possibly more important counterargument, however, is that people
in general may find it more acceptable to try to compensate another
person through public channels directly for a primary good that the
other person lacks in comparison to themselves, than to award that
other person a good or service that they themselves would want but
do not have access to, at least not without devoting their own private
energies to obtaining it. This reduces once more to considerations of
desert. For example, Le Grand and New's severely handicapped person
lacks health, a primary good, compared to, say, the typical person in
society, and it might generally be held that the former thus deserves
to be compensated for that misfortune with the provision of publicly
financed health care; however, he does not necessarily lack nor more
deserve the means to finance global travel compared to the typical
person (who, without a great deal of personal effort, does not have
those means either), and thus the latter may be less supportive of
cross-subsidising that desire.

Regarding Le Grand and New's second point – i.e. their claim
that no-one calls for a National Food Service – we can counter by
returning to the point that without government intervention people
would not be able to organise themselves to provide a decent level of,
say, health or educational services for all members of society, due to
such factors as informational deficiencies, the fact that the need for
these services is sometimes sudden, unexpected and high cost, and
challenges to private collective action.[12] A decent level of basic nutrition – relatively cheap in most countries and highly predictable – does
not tend to suffer so starkly from these issues, particularly in wealthier nations, and basic nutrition can therefore be more assuredly left to
people to provide for themselves via their private actions.[13]

Although health care, education, social care and income support programmes are obvious candidates (and are at least to some extent already publicly delivered in most countries), it is not my intention in this book to suggest a list of sectors that, for the reasons outlined above, ought to be sponsored by government. As aforementioned, the choice of sectors and the extent to which each is supported will be contextual – dependent on a country's wealth, cost of living, demographic and socioeconomic structure, values and so on – but unlike the various and varied desires that exist across people in the private spheres of their lives, each public sector will have a collective goal or limited set of goals that are considered common across service providers and users.[14] Thus, the set of allowable motivational instruments may differ between the public and private domains. But how so?

A NEED TO COMPETE?

In *On Liberty*, Mill (1859/1969, p.72) wrote: 'To individuality should belong the part of life in which it is chiefly the individual that is interested; to society, the part which chiefly interests society.' As argued above, it has proven difficult to secure decent private provision across the whole of society of some primary goods and services that interest individuals *and* society; government intervention is normally required to correct the deficiencies of the private market in this respect. Collective action is required if a collective good, such as health from health care or literacy from education, is to be supplied to all who need it; incentivising egoism risks undermining that liberal objective.

Given that public sector services have single – or limited – collective objectives, the respect that liberals must give to individual autonomy over private objectives is lessened. In the development of public sector services that gathered pace in many countries after the Second World War, such respect was indeed largely absent. It was assumed that the professionals who delivered those services were predominantly public-spirited altruists, fully committed to delivering collectively agreed-upon objectives to the best of their abilities, and that the users of health care, education (etc.) services were accepting of the health and education outcome indicators that the professionals strove to achieve and improve upon.

Over recent decades, however, the assumption that public sector professionals are predominantly altruistically motivated has been disputed by those who argue that these personnel are at the mercy of the mix of motivational forces that are intrinsic to human nature. More specifically, they contend that professionals are often motivated by egoism, and therefore public sector institutions ought to be designed so that this egoism is channelled to serve the common good: to wit, the collectively agreed-upon objectives. Those who adopted this position tended to be influenced heavily by standard notions of economic rationality; they believed that egoism in market exchange drives optimal efficiency, and thus that competitive market incentives ought to be embedded in public sector services.

Perhaps the most prominent early example of the above line of argument was offered by the economist Alain Enthoven (1985) with respect to the UK's National Health Service.[15] However, it was not until the 1990s that the arguments were laid out with reference to intrinsic human motivational drivers, and how these ought to align with institutional design if one is to improve the performance of public sector staff. Le Grand (1997) contended that since egoism, which he alluded to as our knavish instinct, is common, then government ministers and planners ought to take advantage of it by introducing and extending demand-led competitive forces in the public sector.[16] Le Grand's argument was that if providers are required to compete with each other, then they will have an incentive to perform better against the collectively agreed-upon objectives of their public sector service in order to attract users, so as to maintain and increase that which egoistically concerns them – i.e. their revenues. Institutions built upon the assumption that the people working within them are entirely altruistic will, according to Le Grand, incentivise laziness, because their egoism will cause them to be guided by the realisation that their revenues are unaffected by their efforts.

However, if we recall Smith's (1776/1999) illustrative example involving the butcher, the baker and the brewer, we will remember that self-regarding egoism is only likely to be consistent with an optimum outcome for all parties to an exchange over relatively simple goods (and services) delivered by self-employed persons, where there is relatively little room for exploiting market imperfections. If we relax the assumption of self-employment, there are perhaps categories of public sector services where these conditions more or less hold; for example, simple literacy-level indicators for infants, refuse collection, road repairs, many dental procedures, and possibly even routine low-risk medical procedures such as cataract and hernia operations. But it is the contention here that nurturing egoism via a demand-led competitive market is potentially highly detrimental to the objectives of complex public sector services, riven, as they are, by market failures. As illustrated, for instance, by Akerlof and Shiller (2015), in services where there are substantial information asymmetries between providers and consumers, or where there is potential for providers to exploit the behavioural influences for their own advantage, supply-side egoists often act upon their instincts. It is admittedly not inevitable that people will take advantage of these opportunities, but demand-side competition incentivises a dog-eat-dog attitude that encourages people to seek an advantage, and some may resort to pernicious means to do so. Those who succumb to their egoistic tendencies in these circumstances may drive those who might otherwise be more public-spirited to do likewise, or face difficulties in securing revenues.

The political economy of behavioural public policy proposed in this book rules out demand-side competition in the provision of complex public sector services. Indeed, since it is a concern that a constitution built for knaves drives out knightly motivations, my framework warns against the use of such market-style incentives in the provision of simple public sector services also, because one would want to avoid the possibility of incentivised egoism in one domain from becoming a generalised ethos. Public sector services are there by design in large part because they are meant to deliver a single or limited number of collectively agreed-upon goals – to deliver primary goods that are broadly held as foundational if people are to have a reasonable opportunity to pursue their multifarious privately held desires (as well as producing outcomes that benefit society). With respect to the public sector, unlike the private sphere of decision-making, there is thus no need to respect individual autonomy in the pursuit of multifarious desires (including the desire to compete for users); it would likely harm the collectively agreed-upon goals to do so. Yet without demand-side choice one may charge that those who are faced with poor-quality public sector services are stuck with providers that have no incentive to improve. Hayek (1944/2001, p.161) wrote that: 'The most effective way of making people accept the validity of the values they are to serve is to persuade them that they are really the same as those which they, or at least the best among them, have always held, but which were not properly understood or recognised before.' To ask for pure altruism is, I contend, to ask for too much, but the best among us have always reciprocated to serve our long-term self-interest. Fortunately, there are reciprocity-informed mechanisms – some of which use forms of competition – that can be employed to incentivise public sector service improvements.

OTHER WAYS

Although, on what I believe to be liberal principles, I recommend against Le Grand's (and others') advocacy for demand-side competition in public sector services, he is surely right to question whether public sector professionals are predominantly motivated by pure altruism, because this is not a common human trait (see my *Reciprocity* book and the references therein). One could make the argument that public sector professionals will be more altruistic if the institutional design is informed by pure altruism and thus crowds in this characteristic. However, sustaining behaviours that are purely altruistic is only likely to be possible if this motivational driver is a deep-rooted and widespread characteristic of the human (or at least, of the public sector professional) psyche. Of course, people do occasionally demonstrate what are at face value unconditionally generous acts, such as those associated with charity and self-sacrifice, and for some people these actions are perhaps driven by genuine pure altruism; but these actions are often performed to enhance one's reputation so as to indicate that one is worthy of esteem and consideration, or due to the belief that one will be rewarded in the afterlife.[17] Moreover, pure altruists will be exploited by egoists, which places them at an evolutionary disadvantage. In short, people, even when they are doing something that is indisputably good, usually want something in return, either now or later. We are reciprocators, and we demand that others are too.

Decentralising decision-making is a way in which to facilitate people in the pursuit of their desires, but as mooted in Chapter 5 it is also important in relation to the delivery of public sector services. Decentralised regional authorities are of course beholden to the collective public sector objectives that have been decided upon at the national or super-regional level. Although the regional authorities ought to be allowed to also to some degree pursue local-specific goals that other regions might not share, in terms of the broader collectively agreed-upon goals as a primary objective, freedom at the local level is not therefore fostered. However, the regional authorities could be given freedom to experiment and innovate with respect to *how* they might best work to achieve those goals. A role for the national government would then be to disseminate across all regions knowledge of local practises that appear to have been particularly successful.[18]

The reciprocity-informed wage and performance management arguments as a means of improving the situation of both employers and employees in the private domain made in Chapter 7 apply also in relation to the public sector, but combined with decentralisation of decision-making, performance management, in the form of reputational competition, could be a particularly effective mechanism to improve targeted, collectively agreed-upon, outcomes. To reiterate, a concern for one's own reputation is entwined with the evolution of indirect reciprocity because people want to signal to others that they are worthy of their attention, esteem and cooperation. If a national government instituted league tables of regional performance against the collective public sector objectives and disseminated the tables to the general public on, say, an annual basis, each region for each sector would be faced with a reputational incentive to sustain or improve its performance against the various objectives without any need for demand-side competition.[19] Admittedly, such a mechanism may also incentivise the egoistically inclined to misreport their performance, but since the potential to lose resources is absent the incentives to exploit informational asymmetries, compared to those that exist within a demand-led market, are lessened.

Reciprocity and desert are not only relevant to the consideration of how public sector improvements might be incentivised; sustaining public support for public sector services far into the future might determine whether or not those services substantively continue to exist, and thus it would perhaps be wise to inform the design of their basic structure – in relation to who is prioritised or even gets access to the services given constrained budgets – with features that most people support, or at least accept. As alluded to in Chapter 6, Le Grand (1991) mooted the possibility that those who had done nothing continually and knowingly to harm their health might generally be considered a higher priority for public sector health care treatment if in need than those who had, over many years, engaged in health-harming behaviours. The implied reciprocation here is negative: the undeserving unhealthy living would be, in a sense, punished for their perceived bad behaviour.

However, assigning the degree to which a person is responsible for his health misfortunes is not easy. Indeed, it may often be impossible – even lifelong smokers may attribute their lung disease, perhaps in many cases legitimately, to genetics rather than their habit or addiction, for example (and then there is the question of whether people should be held accountable for an addiction). Moreover, when people are severely ill or injured, unless their irresponsibility is extreme, deprioritising them for treatment on the basis of their personal actions, behaviours and choices might be inconsistent with general societal sensibilities, not least because most people might reasonably be able to imagine themselves in a similar position of need. In short, maybe for most of us other considerations trump thoughts on how people in need of health care have lived their lives when prioritising people for treatment, possibly because, no matter what a person does, it is unusual for others to proclaim that they deserve to be ill. However, for those whose behaviours have a reasonably firm link to their predicament – the alcoholic in need of a liver transplant, for example – treatment does usually come with an element of expected reciprocation. We collectively may feel less inclined to treat a person again in the future unless he modifies the behaviours that (probably) caused him to seek treatment in the first place.

Notions of reciprocity and desert may, however, align more immediately and prominently with general sentiments in the provision of some other public services and programmes, at least those unlike, for example, street lighting, that are in principle excludable. As discussed in Chapter 6, an obvious example is income support programmes for working-age people, where one might reasonably contend that beneficiaries ought to reciprocate some hours of public service each week in order to deserve the support that they publicly receive, if, of course, they are physically and mentally able to do so. As aforementioned, not everyone will agree with this proposition, but by informing the design of public institutions and programmes with the core motivational characteristics that drive human behaviour, and by explaining clearly to the public how they are designed as such, we stand a better chance of maintaining the public support for these services that is probably going to be necessary to sustain them at meaningful levels in the decades to come.

For the final substantive comment in this chapter, let us return briefly to the notion of soft and hard forms of paternalism as means of improving public sector service-related outcomes. To reiterate from

Chapter 2, the anti-paternalistic stance in this book applies only to adults who are adjudged to have full agency over their decisions, and thus mandating children to go to school and the institutionalisation of those who present an unreasoned threat to themselves, for example, are allowed. The question, really, is that since the goals of public sector services have been collectively decided upon a priori, is it allowable to manipulate or coerce adults of sound mind into actions that may serve these ends, with respect entirely to those targeted for behaviour change, within the confines of these services? If a significant externality concern is motivating the justification for an intervention – for example, if the intervention is intended to encourage people to wash their hands more frequently or to receive a vaccination, or to discourage people from sending texts or answering their phones during class time, or to make it more likely that they place their rubbish inside rather than next to communal bins – then manipulation and even coercion is warranted. Moreover, it may be reasonable to manipulate or coerce service providers to undertake actions that are likely to serve the goals of public sector services, because the interventions are intended to serve other people – i.e. the service users.[20] But the externality concerns in all of the above rule out the labelling of these interventions as paternalistic (or, strictly speaking, as nudges or shoves). It is my contention that if there are no harms imposed on others then service users deserve full agency over their actions and behaviours. Service users can of course be advised or educated, but if manipulative or coercive tactics are employed they may not agree with what they are being moved towards doing and yet have insufficient recourse to do otherwise; other considerations that are important to them may supersede – for them – any improvement in the principal general objectives of the public sector service in question.

To conclude this chapter, I hope it is clear that the justification that I offer for public sector services – i.e. as means of enhancing freedom by giving more people access to services that produce primary goods that in turn ultimately help them to pursue their own desires – sits well with the liberal tradition. However, given the complexity of public sector services and the potential for the supply side to exploit market failures and the behavioural influences for their own interests, and given that it is less necessary to respect a multitude of desires when there are collectively agreed-upon principal public sector objectives, employing the demand-led competitive market risks introducing harms – without recourse to other positive autonomy-related considerations – that some liberals have tended to underplay. In order for public sector services to best achieve the objectives for which they were in large part established, it is contended here that this market mechanism be disallowed in favour of more direct incentives for purchasers, providers and users to reciprocate. Moreover, if public support is to be sustained for these services into the future, it might be wise for policy makers to clearly articulate how their overall design is informed by motivational characteristics – namely, reciprocity and desert – that most humans are willing to accept.[21]

FOOD FOR THOUGHT

1. Is the pursuit of a collectively agreed-upon goal consistent with supporting freedom?
2. What are the arguments for and against a publicly financed food service?
3. Should there be a demand-led competitive market in public sector services?

9   The Lives of Others

In his book on the evolutionary origins of morality, Boehm (2012, p.273) wrote:

> Critically important are the underlying generous feelings that help a system of indirectly reciprocated meat-sharing to be invented and maintained. Yet it's also true that basically these altruistic tendencies are so moderate that hunter-gatherer sharing institutions need continuous and strong positive cultural support if cooperative benefits are to be reaped without undue conflict. In a sense, then, these innately generous tendencies are not quite up to the job. To finish the job at the cultural level, the serious and continuous threat of group disapproval and active sanctioning does its part in making systems of indirect reciprocity among non-kin work without too much conflict.

Boehm was essentially arguing that the positive reciprocal instincts that evolved to benefit the group – and, by extension, the individuals who comprise the group – will only take us so far, and that the egoism that probably still resides in most of us to varying degrees will cause some people to continue to act entirely selfishly if they think they can get away with it. Therefore, in order to deter egoism, the threat of punishment – and the actual act of punishment if people transgress – is required to complement the almost innate drive for people to reciprocate if all of those who comprise the group are to be given a reasonable opportunity to flourish as they themselves desire.[1]

My position in this book is that people ought to be given a great deal of freedom over how they live their lives so that they can pursue their own desires as they see fit. It is, I contend, a liberal position. However, I acknowledge quite forcefully that when affording people substantial freedom there is a risk that those driven by egoism will attempt to exploit others, or, at the very least, may pay insufficient attention to the circumstances of others, due to their own selfish inclinations. As such, I also contend that these inclinations ought to be countered with interventions that make them less likely to be acted upon, which will inevitably place restrictions on some freedoms. In short, as noted in Chapter 1, in order to protect freedom for all – in order to provide a degree of security from being harmed – we need to curtail some specific freedoms, a position on which all who identify themselves as liberals are unlikely to concur (or, at least, are unlikely to accept restrictions to the extent that I propose).

For instance, as noted in Chapter 8, some of the members of the Austrian School, while believing that an efficient and broadly beneficial economy is driven by cooperation and fair reciprocal exchange, did not appear to acknowledge sufficiently the substantive harms that the market can incentivise – for example, when employers, driven by their own egoism or acting out of necessity in response to the egoism of others, attempt to cut costs by lowering wages and the quality of working conditions. It is this apparent unqualified faith in the market that has fuelled the critics of liberalism and led to the label of neoliberalism being attached to an egoistic *laissez faire* world view of economic, and even social, relationships, although, as also emphasised earlier in this book, egoism is a motivation that most liberals disdain.

To be fair to even the most free-market-minded of the Austrians, their support for their own world view was not entirely unqualified. For instance, von Mises (1927/2005), like Hayek (1944/2001), acknowledged that the free market is not perfect, but contended that it is the only workable system that allows people to attain the ends for which they strive, which, in an economic setting, he assumed to be prosperity, abundance and material well-being. By aspiring to and achieving these ends, he argued, people will engage in social cooperation, their suffering will be alleviated and their happiness enhanced.[2] Von Mises (1927/2005, p.51) considered the notion of a regulated market, explicitly labelling it as a 'third way' between the free market and socialism, but ultimately dismissed it as too damaging to economic efficiency.

Von Mises was concerned that, with regulation, governments might impose on their citizens their own goals that few people would freely wish to follow, and over the private domain of individual decision-making, this is a concern that should not be lightly dismissed. Von Mises argued that his conception of liberalism does not favour the established wealth or special interests that might have an undue influence on government policy. While he was surely right to worry about these potential influences, it is the contention here that he underplayed the power that can be wielded by certain parties in an exchange relationship either directly (by, for example, setting wages and working conditions) or indirectly (by, for instance, exploiting market failures and the behavioural influences) in an unregulated market. Purely from a behavioural perspective, one party to an exchange could, via, for example, carefully designed advertising, use the behavioural influences in order to manipulate other parties. If this happens, a free and fair exchange has been undermined, and the manipulated parties may well now end up purchasing more of a product or service than they desire.[3]

As we know, Mill believed that in certain circumstances the balance of argument did indeed justify government regulations against external harms. In *On Liberty*, for instance, he wrote that:

> Encroachment on [people's] rights; infliction on them of any loss or damage not justified by his own rights; falsehood or duplicity in dealing with them; unfair or ungenerous use of advantages over them; even selfish abstinence from defending them against injury – these are fit objects of moral reprobation, and, in grave cases, of moral retribution and punishment.
>
> *(Mill, 1859/1969, p.75)*[4]

Although Mill did not recognise explicitly the behavioural influences, many of his concerns regarding harms listed in the above passage also inform my political economy of behavioural public policy, but before considering these in greater depth it ought to be acknowledged that neither Mill's nor my approaches contend that all externalities ought to be regulated against (or regulated for, in the case of positive externalities). After all, one could argue that almost every act – perhaps almost every utterance – will be noxious, even if only to a small degree, to someone, and thus if all harms were forbidden or punished, people may feel safe if most of their privately held views were never aired in public.[5] When deciding whether a particular action or behaviour ought to be regulated against from a behavioural perspective, a number of considerations must be balanced against each other.

WHEN TO REGULATE?

It is likely that all real and imaginable government regulations against harms will impose their own harms on someone. Even sensible regulations, such as vehicle speed limits, for instance, will on occasion cause some people to be late for work, and harms that are perceived but that cannot be objectively discerned are still, arguably, harms. Moreover, as we saw in Chapter 6, a harm that is unintended, although not as blameworthy as an intentional harm, cannot be dismissed entirely. More specifically, many commentators, including the disciples of the Austrian School, argue that regulation can stifle innovation, distort priorities, prioritise government interests over those of the citizenry and impose unnecessary barriers to efficiency. In short, regulations involve trade-offs between broadly perceived costs and benefits, and when deliberating on their imposition careful consideration ought to be given on whether the former outweigh the latter.

With respect to behavioural public policy, it is my contention here that if one uses the behavioural influences to harm another party, then it is legitimate to at least consider whether this use should be regulated against, which, if so, would be a form of negative reciprocity.[6] Some may contend that aiming to protect the interests of one party to an exchange from the manipulations of the other party is, in fact, a form of paternalism and is not externality driven at all, because it is to distrust that the first party cannot secure for himself his own best interests. Indeed, as noted in Chapter 3, this form of intervention, where the actions of one party are interfered with to benefit another party in a voluntary two-party exchange, is sometimes labelled "indirect paternalism", because, it is argued, the emphasis is on correcting the first party's misjudgement rather than curtailing the second's party's nefariousness. Here, with respect to my political economy of behavioural public policy, I must disagree, because the primary emphasis is not upon how much of a good or service that anyone chooses to buy, but is instead on the importance of securing an environment for free and fair decision-making, untainted by coercive or manipulative elements. In short, the emphasis is indeed upon curtailing the second party's nefariousness – i.e. to prevent harms.

If we focus for a moment on the relationship between producers and purchases of goods and services, it probably goes without saying that companies and other entities use multifarious marketing tactics and gimmicks to encourage people to purchase their products, and there may be little support or justification for regulating against many of these efforts, even in cases where they are informed by the behavioural influences. For instance, the manufacturers of breakfast cereals might use bright, attractive, anthropomorphic figures on their packaging, which may entice people in the moment to buy more of those products than they otherwise would. Even though the figures are not in themselves educative of what the cereals contain, so long as they do not actively misinform their use might generally be viewed as a relatively harmless infringement on the exchange relationship, intended mainly to get the product noticed in a crowded marketplace. If, on the other hand, the behavioural influences are used to mislead people substantively about the quality, price or implications of purchasing and/or using a product or service, then the argument in favour of regulating against those practices is strengthened. For example, if payday loan companies, which typically issue short-term loans at high rates of interest, were to highlight the joys of spending and to underplay the pain of repayment (and misled with respect to the interest rate charged), the general conclusion might be that their interference in the exchange relationship is excessive and that their activities in this respect ought to be constrained.

Admittedly, the point at which regulation is favoured is something of a grey area, but to reiterate, the primary focus in relation to the political economy of behavioural public policy proposed here is on interference in the exchange relationship, not on whether a good or service is deemed a good or bad thing to purchase from a particular paternalistic perspective. For instance, let us consider two consumables – say, cigarettes and lettuces – the former potentially harmful to health and the latter typically not. Without any behavioural-informed manipulative marketing tactics, some people will still consume cigarettes because, for them, the benefits they get from smoking outweigh the harms (i.e. smoking remains one of their desires), and many people will of course continue to consume lettuces. In such circumstances the purchase of these two products is the result of a free and fair exchange and from the behavioural perspective offered here there are no grounds for government interference. An anti-smoker might not like the fact that some people still smoke, but if smokers are imposing no harms on other people then there is no justification to regulate smoking either on the demand side or supply side because to do so would be to impact on other people's personal desires.[7]

However, if the producers of cigarettes and lettuces use the behavioural influences to manipulate people into purchasing more of these products than they would otherwise desire, then we would witness an infringement upon the notion of a free and fair exchange in these markets. In such circumstances, regulation is potentially, although not definitely, warranted; the strength of the case for regulation would need to be considered on a market-by-market basis. The interference from producers in both markets would be motivated by their own egoism and therefore ought to be scrutinised, but the case for regulating the cigarette manufacturers might be viewed as stronger than that for regulating the suppliers of lettuces because, in the former, consumers may be induced to accept more potential health-related harms than they, in the absence of manipulation, desire, and as discussed in Chapter 8, health can be considered a primary good that impacts on our potential to pursue many of our other desires. In many countries, cigarettes are also expensive, and thus there are financial implications of purchasing more of them than one really wants. The consumption of an extra lettuce or two each week is unlikely to have such serious potential health implications (and with this product being quite cheap, it would unlikely have a notable impact on consumers' financial situation also). Thus, the broad conclusion might be to turn a blind eye to any manipulations by lettuce sellers (within reason).[8]

In the above discussion, the focus is on the parties who are involved directly in the exchange relationship; specifically, consideration is given to the possibility that one of those parties imposes externalities on the other by manipulating the exchange relationship in their own favour. Unless the party who suffers the externality is being manipulated *entirely* to engage in the exchange – i.e. unless that party, in the absence of manipulation, would choose deliberately not to engage in the exchange at all – then even with the manipulation the trade would to some extent be conducive to the pursuit of his personal desires. For example, if the person were to smoke one packet of cigarettes per week in the absence of manipulation (and, say, two packets a week if manipulated), then we cannot conclude that smoking one packet, even with manipulation, is inconducive to his personal desires. We can, however, surmise that smoking the extra packet is not something that he really wants to do and may therefore impact negatively on the pursuit of his desires.[9] Thus, when considering the externalities that might arise from behavioural-informed manipulation to the parties that are directly involved in the exchange relationship, behavioural regulation would rarely call for an outright ban on that activity. It would, at most, call for a ban on the offending manipulation, and, as suggested, the only times that it would be consistent with an outright ban is if the person being manipulated, in the absence of manipulation, decided to take no part in the exchange.

That being said, in economics the more common conception of a negative externality occurs to a third party – a party who does not participate directly in the exchange relationship. As alluded to in note 7, consideration of these third-party negative externalities would further strengthen the case for behavioural regulation if a manipulated exchange between two parties were imposing substantive negative externalities on a third party, since the third party would be feeling consequences that may in turn negatively affect the potential for him to pursue his own desires in life, and yet he would be reaping none of the benefits of the exchange. However, although the argument for regulation against behavioural manipulation would be strengthened in these circumstances, the remit of behavioural public policy again rarely extends to a complete ban on the activity, because the exchange relationship between the principal partners would still normally exist, if perhaps to a lesser extent, if it were freely and fairly determined. Therefore, if third-party negative externalities are significant enough to justify a complete ban on a free and fair exchange relationship, this would fall within the remit not of behavioural public policy, but of public policy more broadly defined.[10]

I have elsewhere termed applications of behavioural-informed regulation "budges" (mentioned in Chapter 2); this is a good place to consider the parameters of budging in a little more depth (Oliver, 2013, 2015, 2017).

DEFINING BUDGES

Within the field of behavioural public policy, budge interventions are conceptually the polar opposite of nudges. Specifically, the latter are liberty-preserving and – as signalled by the *paternalism* within libertarian paternalism – (ought to) target internalities, whereas the former are explicitly regulatory and target externalities.[11] There is, however, a form of behavioural public policy intervention that falls between these conceptual poles that are typically mislabelled as nudges (with the term sometimes prefixed by the word "social"). It is misleading to attach the nudge label to these interventions as they are not instruments of paternalism. They are, like nudges, liberty-preserving, but they target externalities, and therefore in the interests of intellectual clarity they ought to be given a label that delineates them from other types of behavioural intervention. I label them here as "steers".

In practice, steers are probably more common than nudges, perhaps partly because people might find it more acceptable for governments or other bodies of authority to manipulate their behaviours if they believe the motivation for doing so is to reduce harms to others rather than to reduce harms to oneself. To place green footprints on the ground that lead in the direction of rubbish receptacles is an example of a steer, since it is behaviourally informed (i.e. impacting perhaps on present bias, and influencing through salience), is principally motivated to reduce the harm felt by others from being exposed to litter, and yet can be ignored if those targeted are unreceptive. Setting a default on a classroom heating system is another example of a steer intervention: the preset default itself is the behavioural aspect, its setting at a relatively low temperature is aimed at the negative externality of excessive energy use, and yet the temperature can easily be turned up if one is too cold. Budges are more forceful than steers and are not, therefore, so easy to override or ignore. They often impose the threat of negative reciprocity rather than offer a guiding hand. They are not intended to be liberty-preserving. Hence their placement at point D in the behavioural public policy cube depicted in Figure 2.1 of Chapter 2; a pure steer, on the other hand, would be placed at point E.[12]

As detailed in the previous section, behavioural-informed manipulations that undermine a free and fair exchange and which thus impose negative externalities upon one of the parties to that exchange are potential grounds for introducing a budge intervention, and the justification for such an intervention is strengthened if the manipulated exchange imposes externalities on third parties. But there are also other grounds for budging. To return to Mill (1859/ 1969, p.14):

> There are ... many positive acts for the benefit of others, which [the individual] may rightly be compelled to perform; such as to give evidence in a court of justice; to bear his fair share in the common defence, or in any other joint work necessary to the interest of the society of which he enjoys the protection; and to perform certain acts of individual beneficence, such as saving a fellow-creatures life, or interposing to protect the defenceless against ill-usage, things which whenever it is obviously a man's duty to do, he may rightfully be made responsible to society for not doing. A person may cause evil to others not only by his actions but by his inaction, and in either case he is justly accountable to them for the injury.

There are occasions when the behavioural influences cause individual inertia, and where it is assumed that the default position that people are faced with is consistent with the pursuit of their desires. However, although many people perhaps have a desire to be inert, they may largely be indifferent to the position that this places them in, so long as an altered position is more or less costless to them – and yet that altered position may offer great benefits to others.

To illustrate, assume that the default on organ donor registration in a particular country is that people are required to register to be a donor, which is known as an opt-in system. In such a system, many people who do not object to being a donor are, via a status quo effect, unlikely to register and yet their failure to do so has serious negative potential implications for the health, and the lives, of others.[13] In short, the potential forgone external benefits equate to serious potential external harms. If the organ donor registration system was changed to one of presumed consent – or opt-out – those people who did not previously opt in and yet would not object to being a donor, are now registered, and their organs, in the event of their death, can potentially be used to improve the health and to save the lives of others. They would still of course be required to do nothing with respect to organ donor registration, and thus their desire to be inert is unaffected (and there would be no substantive costs imposed on most of them), but the position that they are now placed in helps to realise otherwise foregone external benefits, which equates to reducing external harms.

Changing the default from opt-in to opt-out in the expectation that it would change the outcome regarding the number of people who are registered as potential donors is informed by a knowledge of behavioural science; it would require an act of legislation and does not preserve liberty because the option of opting in is no longer available (and some people, unaware of the change in the default, would essentially be coerced into being a donor); and, as we have seen, its motive would be to address externalities. Given all this, and although changing the default for organ donation is typically mislabelled as a nudge, we can see quite clearly that it is in fact a budge.[14] Now that (I hope) we all know what a budge is, let us consider a few more illustrative examples of this type of behavioural intervention in action.

ILLUSTRATING BUDGES

Countless examples of potentially beneficial budges could be described, but space constraints limit me to a further five illustrative examples that I hope will dispel any lingering doubt about what budges entail.

1. To start with another intervention that is often mischaracterised as a nudge, through long experience the marketing divisions of confectionary companies know that salience and immediacy can have a substantial impact on consumer buying patterns. Consequently, they have traditionally paid supermarkets to have their products displayed at child eye level near to checkout counters. If we conclude that this practice potentially manipulates people into buying more confectionary and unhealthy snacks than they otherwise would, then policy makers have an intellectual justification to regulate against the activity. A *regulation* against the negative externality of a behavioural-informed manipulation is a budge.

2. Similarly, supermarkets are often financially induced to place alcoholic beverages at the end of shopping aisles since it is known that the salient positioning of products increases sales (by as much as a price reduction of 4–9 per cent, according to Nakamura *et al.*, 2014). If it was concluded that the end-of-aisle placement, which is motivated by the egoism of the supermarkets and the alcoholic drinks industry, was manipulating consumers unduly, and that this interference was therefore impinging negatively on a free and fair exchange, there would be a behavioural justification for regulating openly against the practice. The regulation would thus also meet all of the budge criteria.[15]

3. The money savings expert Martin Lewis observed that his local supermarket was selling single packs of Jaffa Cakes (each containing ten cakes) next to double packs (containing twenty cakes), with both pack sizes priced at £1.[16] This is an example of what behavioural economists have termed the decoy effect, where retailers offer a choice of items with one of those items being a relatively bad deal, in the expectation that the other item will now appear almost too attractive to resist. In the absence of the decoy, it might be that most consumers who bought the item when the decoy was present would not wish to buy the good or service at all, and therefore the introduction of the decoy potentially impacts negatively on a free and fair exchange. With respect to Lewis's example, a person might not really want any Jaffa Cakes, but with the decoy will be manipulated into buying twenty of them. If we believe that this behavioural manipulation interferes unacceptably in the exchange mechanism, we have a justification for budging against the use of decoys.

4. High street and online gambling outlets are particularly well suited for exploiting the behavioural influences, because people tend to anchor on the jackpot prizes, are overoptimistic with respect to the objective probability of winning and, as we saw in Chapter 1, chase losses with ever more risk-seeking choices.[17] Responsible gambling may of course be a safe, enjoyable activity for a great many people and is thus likely to reflect their considered desires, but if the exchange relationship is manipulated unduly – as it often is – then the gambling industry has the capability of inflicting serious harms. Humans seek to learn from and to emulate people whom they admire, a phenomenon called the prestige effect, which, from an evolutionary perspective, is understandable, because seeking to learn from

those who are most respected is likely to aid survival and reproductive successes. Unfortunately, this ingrained trait now causes many to be influenced unduly by sports, showbusiness, reality television and social media celebrities. Using celebrities to market products and services is nothing new of course, but specifically with respect to the online gambling industry it is being an increasingly visible marketing strategy. We may wonder why millionaires do not self-regulate rather than use their celebrity to earn yet more money and, via the prestige effect, to manipulate poor people to impoverish themselves further. But since that it is evidently asking too much the budge framework again offers policy makers an intellectual justification for regulating against the use of influencers for these purposes.

5. The risk and decision analysts Robert Meyer and Howard Kunreuther wrote in their book, *The Ostrich Paradox*, that:

> The Diphtheria-Tetanus-Pertussis [Pertussis is whooping cough] (DTP) combination vaccine had been routinely used for more than 20 years, so that whooping cough had become a much less common disease in comparison with its incidence in the mid-20 century. In January 1974, however, an article described 36 children who were claimed to have suffered severe neurological complications following their DTP immunization. It reported that the vaccine was only marginally effective, and questioned whether its benefits outweighed the risks. Television documentaries and newspaper reports dramatized tragic stories of profoundly intellectually disabled children allegedly injured by the vaccine …. The result of all this negative publicity was a rapid fall in the immunization rates against whooping coughs … pertussis epidemics followed, leading to the deaths of some children.
>
> (Meyer and Kunreuther, 2017, pp. 63–64)

The media are of course egoistically incentivised to sensationalise, because a dramatic depiction of circumstances and events tends to boost viewing and circulation figures, but when reporting on vaccinations, anchoring upon the potential costs without sufficient attention to their benefits may harm those (or the children of those) who might otherwise choose to vaccinate. In the case of infectious diseases, this may also generate further negative externalities to third parties. A budge here might therefore be to regulate so that news stories that depict the potential harms of any vaccination programme must also give an appropriate degree of attention to the harms of not vaccinating (and vice versa).

To conclude, if one is to allow people a great deal of freedom over how they live their lives, then one can expect that some will act upon their egoistic instincts to attempt to obtain an unfair or exploitative advantage at the expense of others. Some of those attempts will use the behavioural influences, either implicitly or explicitly, to distort the exchange relationship. These activities comprise a subset of what Akerlof and Shiller (2015) term phishing and what Sunstein (2020) and others have labelled sludge. But the behavioural influences can also cause people with less malign intentions to impose harms on others in the form of what would be easily won but ultimately forgone external benefits, as might be seen when individuals are influenced and impacted heavily by inertia.

Thus, in addition to fostering positive reciprocity, my political economy of behavioural public policy calls for regulation to mitigate behavioural-informed negative externalities (i.e. as a form of negative reciprocity) and for behavioural-informed positive externalities, an approach that I have labelled budge. There are countless potential budges and some illustrative examples were summarised above, but this is not to argue that every budge ought to be implemented.[18] They would need to be considered case-by-case, and only those activities that are generally adjudged to have breached some level of unacceptability will be regulated against (or for), with such factors as harms to third as well as second parties to an exchange, whether the harms imposed by the activity negatively affect what might be considered primary goods, and how intrusive it really is in terms of impacting liberty when moving people from one default position to another, all adding grist to the mill when one is considering whether or not to budge.

Ultimately, although not all potential budges will meet the requirements for implementation, the approach provides a behavioural-informed intellectual justification for when regulation might be appropriate in particular circumstances. Budge regulation should never be seen as arbitrary; it should always be seen as befitting – or as deserving of – the "crime".

FOOD FOR THOUGHT

1. Should there be laws against harmful free speech?
2. If one person is harmed by another's inertia, should the latter be forced to act?
3. Can there ever be a free and fair exchange between two or more parties?

10 **Summing Up**

This short final chapter concludes not only this book, but the trilogy of books that I have in recent years written on the origins, development and future of at least one important branch of behavioural public policy, a future that I hope will place this relatively new sub-field of public policy firmly in the liberal tradition. I will begin by reiterating part of the Introduction – i.e. by summarising the arguments that I have presented in the preceding pages – before offering some final thoughts.

HOW I ARRIVED HERE

The political economy of behavioural public policy that I propose is anti-paternalistic. I make no apology for that. You are either a paternalist or you are not. I personally have no urge to interfere in the lives of those who are imposing no harms on others – beyond that of attempting to educate and inform – and I do not desire others to interfere in mine (a reciprocity of sorts). This represents a radical departure from the conceptual policy frameworks that have thus far dominated the field, which have principally consisted of soft forms of paternalism, but have also extended to harder, more coercive forms of paternalism, advocated by those who believe that the softer forms will ultimately prove insufficiently effective.

Some of my fellow supposedly liberal-minded scholars who have expressed their support for soft forms of paternalism have done so by referring to four limitations of human reasoning ability; specifically, limitations on imagination, willpower, objectivity and technical ability. Le Grand and New (2015), for instance, express the view that these limitations offer a legitimate justification for state paternalism over individual actions that might cause harms to self in the distant future and over actions that have a small chance of an immediate catastrophic outcome. Libertarian paternalists go beyond this quite restricted pair of circumstances in their support for soft paternalism, but like Le Grand and New they appear to base their conclusions on the argument that individuals sometimes fail themselves in the pursuit of that for which they ought to be striving – specifically, more welfare, utility or happiness – and are thus in need of the guiding hand of the policy maker.

However, I questioned whether utility (or welfare or happiness) maximisation is a legitimate ubiquitous normative goal; indeed, in the history of economic thought no consensus has been reached on what utility even is. Hume, for instance, aligned utility with public usefulness, Bentham with hedonic feelings of pleasure and pain, and Mill and modern welfare economists with pretty much anything. Some equate utility with the eudemonic notion of a worthwhile or meaningful life, and still others with a satisfied life. A possible reason why there are many different definitions attached to the concept of utility is because most people, much of the time, are not, nor wish to be, driven to maximise utility at all, irrespective of how it is defined. That is, the pursuit of utility often does not drive desires, but rather desires are antecedent, and, at most, some conception of utility is a possible consequence of achieving one's desires. Desires are multifarious, vary across and within people, and may, for some, be meaningfully facilitated by the behavioural influences, such as present bias and loss aversion, that outside observers might mistakenly believe are an inevitable cause of biases and errors in judgement.[1] It is thus argued in this book that the policy maker's role in the private realm of individual decision-making should not be to interfere so as to strive to maximise the greatest utility, but rather to put in place general conditions – and institutions – that facilitate people in the pursuit of their own conception of the desired life.

As aforementioned, desires are multifarious (and can include, but are not limited to, the pursuit of any one or more of the various forms of utility) – they differ interpersonally and, over time and context, intra-personally, and their fulfilment makes for a flourishing life. At the heart of the liberal tradition is the assumption that, given the right institutions, the best way to allow people to fulfil their desires is to afford them a great deal of freedom over their actions, principally because this is the most effective means by which to forge the social cooperation from which we all benefit in our own ways. However, unless the reciprocal sentiments that underlie cooperative actions are protected and nurtured, they can wither; three general recommendations to nurture reciprocity are to emphasise its import- ance in the political and policy rhetoric, to tackle income and wealth concentrations, and to decentralise policy decision-making.

It is worth keeping in mind that the urge to reciprocate – both positively and negatively – is driven by perceptions of desert, which lie at the heart of notions of justice and in their raw form are almost instinctive rather than intellectual. For instance, desert appears to drive actions and behaviours not only in very young children, but also perhaps in some non-human species. A person's intentions – towards others and towards himself – and the outcomes that may result from his actions and behaviours, are both associated with the extent to which a person is considered deserving of reward or admonishment. Given the importance that people attach to desert, this concept inev- itably underlies our personal private relationships and collaborations; to help sustain adequate public sector services and welfare systems, considerations of desert ought to inform the design of policies, insti- tutions and interventions in those domains also.

Followers of the liberal economic tradition believe that the competitive market is effective at fostering social cooperation and subsequently optimising the opportunities for people to achieve their privately held desires. This viewpoint tends to underplay somewhat the fact that the competitive market presents significant incentives for exchange partners to act upon their egoistic instincts, which may damage the wider group. However, the excesses of the market can be regulated against; moreover, in the domain of private decision-making where people have multifarious desires, the disallowance of the

competitive market would be too much of an infringement on autonomy from any liberal perspective. However, aside from regulating
against any excessive harms that the market might cause, governments have a legitimate role to play in encouraging free and fair
private exchange and transactions – through the general structuring
of society and via information and education – between employers
and employees, buyers and sellers, and within communities and families.[2] That is, governments can help to provide the conditions that
facilitate each of us to get what we deserve.

Unlike the private domain of individual decision-making,
public sector services are each charged to deliver a limited number
of collectively agreed-upon goals, with these objectives – e.g. health,
literacy, dignity, financial security – being in some sense foundational
if people are to have reasonable opportunities of fulfilling their private
desires. Given that public sector objectives are collectively agreed
upon a priori, respect for autonomy can be to some extent relaxed in
this domain. Moreover, the complexity of many public sector services
lends scope for egoistically inclined suppliers to exploit market failures and the behavioural influences for their own interests. Taking
into account all of the above, my proposed political economy of
behavioural public policy advises against demand-led competitive
markets in the public sector. Instead, it is suggested that purchasers,
providers and users be given alternative incentives to reciprocate, by,
for example, instituting reputational competition between service
suppliers. Moreover, and as suggested earlier, in order to sustain
substantive public sector services and welfare programmes far into
the future, it is argued that their design and application ought to be
informed by notions of reciprocity and desert – i.e. motivational
characteristics that most people intrinsically accept.

I have issued a call that people be given a great deal of freedom
over how they live their lives. Unfortunately, in and of itself, such a
proposal lends much scope for the egoistically inclined to act upon
their instincts by seeking advantage at the expense of others. Where
those attempts use the behavioural influences to further their aims

(by distorting the exchange relationship), or indeed where the behavioural influences cause others to forgo what could be easily won benefits, there exists an intellectual justification for behavioural-informed regulation – or, in other words, for budge interventions. Therefore, overall, my political economy of behavioural public policy has two arms: the first arm proposes that policy makers foster the desert-based positive reciprocity that most people almost innately accept, so as to give each person a better chance of fulfilling their own personal desires in life; and the second arm calls for regulating those who might otherwise take advantage of their freedom by (implicitly or explicitly) using the behavioural influences to impose harms on others.

AND FINALLY...

No claim is made here that my political economy of behavioural public policy, if followed, will liberate all untapped potential or solve all of society's ills – no approach to behavioural public policy can do that. For example, tackling climate change – probably the most profound policy challenge that we all face – needs heavy regulation against harms on a global scale that falls outside the realm of behavioural public policy, or at least my preferred version of it. The most significant climate-related harms are probably not caused by some people manipulating others and thereby distorting the exchange relationship. Perfectly deliberate and desired exchanges between, say, suppliers and consumers can lead to great harms to third parties (i.e. the biosphere), some of which might be tackled through better education, but ultimately we would need to regulate against the activities that are causing those harms, further develop alternative less harmful technologies, and assist those who lose out from these regulatory interventions.[3]

Nonetheless, the message of the importance of nourishing reciprocity that runs throughout this book should fundamentally underpin the climate change response: i.e. if you take care of the environment, it will likely take better care of you (and your children and grandchildren). More generally, acting reciprocally in the positive sense is crucial to the functioning of all societies, which ultimately benefits us all. In the novel *Looking Backward*, Dr Leete, in talking to Julian West after the latter's century-long sleep, expressed a similar sentiment when he said that: 'The necessity of mutual dependence should imply the duty and guarantee of mutual support; and that it did not in your day constituted the essential cruelty and unreason of your system' (Bellamy, 1888/1996, p.64). The novel's author, Edward Bellamy, was envisioning a socialist utopia, but socialism risks the curtailment of too many freedoms for mutual dependence to thrive. I contend that a more palatable, and better functioning, representation of his dream is the liberal society.

The notion, often attributed to standard rational choice theory, that most or even all of us pursue our self-interest with no regards for others – i.e. that we are selfish egoists – is not a fair caricature of humankind. People, admittedly to a greater or lesser extent interpersonally, do take account of others' actions and circumstances when deciding, choosing, acting and behaving. To re-emphasise this point, we can turn once more to Hume (1751/2018, p.104), who wrote that: 'Men's inclination, their necessities, lead them to combine; their understanding and experience tell them that this combination is impossible where each governs himself by no rule, and pays no regard to the possessions of others.' Yet a degree of egoism probably resides within most of us, and ought to be curtailed through regulation if necessary, if it threatens the social functionings that have evolved to benefit us all.

I am not overly optimistic about whether the vision offered in this book can be applied in its entirety in practice, because there is no political party, at least in the United Kingdom but I think also in many other countries, that adopts and applies this view of liberalism. Over the last forty years (excepting recent experiences of tackling a global pandemic), Conservatives have leaned increasingly towards libertarianism (at least with respect to supply-side interests), offering too few protections against harms and bowing to those from whom they benefit financially. Those on the left of the political spectrum, who are in some countries misleadingly labelled as liberals, often implicitly embrace a type of authoritarianism by aiming to interfere paternalistically in the minutia of personal private lives with the justification that they know better about what the person desires than does the person himself. Yet I suspect that most of us would embrace a perspective that leaves people free if they are imposing no harms on others while offering protections against those who do indeed impose harms.

On this note, I will leave the final word to John Stuart Mill and the maxims that he outlined in his work, *On Liberty*:

> The maxims are, first, that the individual is not accountable to society for his actions, in so far as these concern the interests of no one but himself. Advice, instruction, persuasion, and avoidance by other people, if thought necessary by them for their own good, are the only measures by which society can justifiably express its dislike or disapprobation of his conduct. Secondly, that for such actions as are prejudicial to the interests of others, the individual is accountable, and may be subjected either to social or to legal punishment, if society is of the opinion that the one or the other is requisite for its protection.
>
> *(1859/1969, p.90)*

Within the limits of behavioural policy, those are my maxims also.

FINAL FOOD FOR THOUGHT

1. Can liberals ever be dismissive of those who disagree with them?
2. Would you vote for a political party that would intervene only to regulate against harms?
3. Are we all liberals at heart?

Notes

PREFACE

1 This book is an elaboration and extension of an article that I published in *Public Administration Review* in 2019 (79: 917–924), titled "Towards a New Political Economy of Behavioural Public Policy".

2 See: www.ft.com/content/670039ec-98f3-11e9-9573-ee5cbb98ed36

3 My arguments are intended to apply only to adults who have full agency over their conduct. I recognise, of course, that paternalistic intervention is often necessary when one is dealing with children or with adults who suffer from certain mental incapacities.

4 Mill did not believe that all acts of egoism merit punishment. For example, there are cases where one might expect people to reciprocate and cooperate, but where they are not morally obliged to do so. He termed these "imperfect obligations" (Mill, 1863/1969).

INTRODUCTION

1 The cover designs of the three books were also meant to be meaningful. The tree diagram on the cover of the *Origins* book was intended to mirror Darwin's famous sketch of the branching system of descent in his notebooks, the golden cog connecting the rest of the mechanism on the cover of the *Reciprocity* book was meant to signify the importance of the golden rule for the full functioning of society, and the tree in bloom on the cover of the current volume represents, in my interpretation at least, a flourishing life.

2 Although behavioural-informed interventions have been implemented by governments and other bodies in a haphazard fashion for many years, behavioural public policy as a recognised subfield of public policy is a little over a decade old at the time of writing, and has been given an identity and structure by the establishment of teams working in universities, local and national governments, non-governmental local, national and international agencies, and private organisations. Formal

overarching political economic behavioural public policy frameworks are still, however, lacking.

3 Even a brief summary of the development of all that can be classified as behavioural science would in and of itself require several volumes.

4 I will revisit some of these frameworks in Chapter 2 of the current book because they serve as contrasts to the political economy of behavioural public policy that I will postulate, and thus, it is hoped, help to clarify how the parameters of my own preferred approach differ from those narrower frameworks that have been principally considered to date.

5 In the *Origins* book, I was not entirely opposed to soft and even hard forms of paternalism in some instances, particularly where the implications for personal lifestyle choice could be viewed as reasonably minor. However, over the years, as will be seen in the current book, my tolerance for paternalism in even those circumstances has weakened, and I prefer that with respect to the internalities of adults of sound mind, policy makers limit themselves to open, explicit educational and informational interventions. I acknowledge, of course, that many governments around the world appear to have given up on the ideal of delivering open objective education (if they ever embraced that ideal in the first place), and that they resort increasingly to fake news and propaganda instead. But my intention in this book is to argue for what (I think) "can and ought to be", and not, unfortunately, what "is".

6 Positive and negative reciprocity can broadly respectively be defined as the in-kind return of kind and unkind intentions/actions/behaviours.

7 A reviewer of a draft manuscript of the current book questioned why I had not referred to the work of Peter Kropotkin (1902/2014), author of the classic text, *Mutual Aid*. Kropotkin shared views in common with some of the classical liberals in that he also believed that a society that was not controlled too heavily by central government would flourish through the then more likely incidence of cooperative activities within communities. However, I referred to Kropotkin quite extensively in my *Reciprocity* book, and I wanted to avoid too much repetition across the three books.

8 Robert Sugden (2018), in his *The Community of Advantage*, perhaps comes closest to offering such an overarching framework.

9 Perhaps I hope for too much.

10 When the occasion calls for it, I have used the terms "he" and "him" rather than "she" and "her". I used the feminine terms in my previous book, and it was thus the turn of the masculine.

CHAPTER I

1 'The purest treasure mortal times afford, Is spotless reputation: that away, Men are but gilded loam or painted clay' (Egan, 1830/2006, p.318).

2 Reciprocity is also central to the economist Robert Sugden's approach in his book, *The Community of Advantage* (Sugden, 2018). Consistent with the approach offered in this book, Sugden concludes that policy makers ought to strive to increase the opportunities over which people can choose rather than express a consequentialist concern for their welfare, but Sugden is less willing to regulate against harms.

3 This will, however, be a brief reflection. For more detailed discussions, see, for example, Oliver (2019) and the references therein.

4 Admittedly, these and other evolutionary theorists are likely to believe that there are multiple legitimate contributing explanations for the origin and strengthening of reciprocal tendencies.

5 The biologist Gerald Wilkinson has observed reciprocation between non-related wild vampire bats following successive food hunts in Costa Rica, seemingly an implicit insurance strategy given the uncertainty of individual success on any particular night (Wilkinson, 1984; Carter and Wilkinson, 2013).

6 In a recent BBC adaptation of *A Christmas Carol* (see, at the time of writing, www.bbc.co.uk/programmes/m000csdp), after being haunted by the three ghosts of Christmas, Ebenezer Scrooge does not decide to seek redemption for personal salvation (he believes that he deserves everything that he has coming to him); rather, he reforms himself solely to save Tiny Tim. This act of pure altruism may appeal to a higher form of morality than a concern for "what's in it for me", but the latter is a stronger evolved human tendency than the former. If Charles Dickens desired that his message might genuinely and generally cause people to address any wrongdoing that they may have committed, the more traditional interpretation of Scrooge's motivation would likely have a more lasting effect.

7 Incidentally, de Tocqueville believed that humans learn to reciprocate and cooperate at a very young age in circumstances where everyone has something that they wish to protect, and that this continues in adulthood. 'When a child begins to move in the midst of the objects that surround him', he wrote,

he is instinctively led to appropriate to himself everything that he can lay his hands upon; he has no notion of the property of others; but as he gradually learns the value of things and begins to perceive that he may in his turn be despoiled, he becomes more circumspect, and he ends by respecting those rights in others which he wishes to have respected in himself. The principle which the child derives from the possession of his toys is taught to the man by the objects which he may call his own.

(de Tocqueville, 1835/1998, p.94)

Admittedly, at least in relation to nineteenth-century Americans, de Tocqueville believed that men (and presumably women) also make sacrifices without any regard for their own self-interest.

8 Hume at this point appears to equate utility with public usefulness rather than hedonic feelings of pleasure and pain. More will be written on the complex subject of utility in Chapter 4.

9 Regarding one of our close cousins, the orangutans, the naturalist and broadcaster David Attenborough wrote that their

preference for solitude may well be connected to their size. Orangs are fruit-eaters, and, being so big, have to find considerable quantities of it every day to sustain themselves. Fruiting trees, however, are uncommon and widely scattered through the forest, at widely varying intervals. Some only bear fruit once every twenty-five years. Others do so almost continuously for about a century but on one branch at a time. Yet others have no regular pattern and are triggered irregularly by a particular change in the weather such as a sudden drop in temperature that precedes a heavy thunderstorm. Even when they do produce fruit, it may only hang on the tree and be edible for a week or so before it becomes over-ripe, falls or is stolen. So the orang have to make long journeys, continually searching, and may well find it more profitable to keep their discoveries to themselves.

(Attenborough, 1979/2019, pp.322–323)

In short, orangutans face extreme scarcity and may have evolved as egoists as a consequence. Given the human disregard for their natural habitat over the decades, we should not expect to discover cooperation among wild orangutans anytime soon. Moreover, scarcity might not need to be real, but merely perceived, for orangutans (and other species) to behave egoistically, as witnessed by panic buying and hoarding by humans during the early days of the Covid-19 pandemic.

10 Food may sometimes be scarce even if the source of the food is abundant if it is difficult to turn the source into food. For instance, if buffalo were abundant but difficult to catch, then buffalo meat might still be scarce. Incidentally, once egoism has prevailed over cooperation it becomes very difficult to reverse this state of affairs, as noted by the political scientist Edward Banfield in his study of a poor rural Italian community in the 1950s (Banfield, 1958). Moreover, Hume, as on most topics in relation to human behaviour, was not silent on this issue, asking us to

> Suppose a society to fall into such want of all common necessaries, that the utmost frugality and industry cannot preserve the greater number from perishing, and the whole from extreme misery; It will readily, I believe, be admitted, that the strict laws of justice are suspended, in such a pressing emergence, and give place to the stronger motives of necessity and self-preservation. Is it any crime, after a shipwreck, to seize whatever means or instrument of safety one can lay hold of, without regard to former limitations of property?
>
> *(Hume, 1751/2018, p.15)*

11 The implication here is that if an individual were to play a gamble a large number of times, such that, on average, he would secure winnings equal to the expected value, he would sacrifice some of his potential winnings in order to avoid the gamble (converse arguments can be made with respect to risk-seeking behaviour, where an individual would want more than the expected value of a gamble for certain in order to reject the risk). The rules of rational choice theory assume that people will be close to indifferent between a gamble and the certainty of its expected value, but these rules implicitly assume that people will be able to repeat the game many times. However, in evolutionary terms (e.g. securing game in a hunt for sustenance over the next few days), and even in the modern world, many decisions may be "one-shot". In such circumstances, one may quite rationally choose to avoid a risky option even if the gamble is heavily weighted in one's favour if resources sufficient for one's needs can be secured without risking anything (or at least, with less risk), and conversely, one might engage in an unpromising risk if the alternative is certain doom. The economist Paul Samuelson (1963) offered a related discussion.

12 For example, in relation to the top right-hand quadrant, if an individual were offered a choice between a gamble that offers a 0.99 chance of losing £1,000 and a 0.01 chance of losing nothing or the gamble's expected loss of £990 for sure, prospect theory predicts that the risky option will be chosen (i.e. risk-seeking behaviour); with respect to the bottom right-hand quadrant, prospect theory predicts that a choice between a gamble that offers a 0.01 chance of losing £1,000 and a 0.99 chance of losing nothing or the gamble's expected loss of £10 for sure would result in a preference for the sure loss (i.e. risk-averse behaviour).

13 That said, simple games of chance are played in some hunter-gatherer societies, although the consideration of well-defined probabilities are unlikely there, and we cannot be sure how far into the past those games were played. For example, the Hadza of Tanzania play lukuchuko, where pieces of bark are thrown to see which side lands facing upwards.

14 It is not that most people fundamentally and consistently like or dislike risk per se; rather, the circumstances that they face guides and sometimes necessitates their particular risk-related behaviours.

15 There are echoes here with the political scientist Herbert Simon's notion that people satisfice rather than maximise (Simon, 1956).

16 Tests of the reflection effect are not designed to uncover pro-social tendencies, but it is possible that the reciprocal instincts evolved in part as an implicit insurance strategy to further improve survival chances when taking risks in times of scarcity. As discussed earlier, however, egoism would likely dominate when people are faced with extreme scarcity.

17 There may be many other explanations for why people decide, act and behave in the ways that they do, but I do not have the space or the knowledge to discuss all of these possible alternatives. My point is simply that there may be reasonable explanations for patterns of decision-making that are often consistent with prospect theory's reflection effect but that do not necessarily imply that a person's responses are biased.

18 Most of us pay insurance premiums that do not take us too far away from our anticipated levels of wealth in order to mitigate against disaster.

19 If one were to alter the magnitude of the outcomes used, the extent to which prospect theory's predicted reflection effect is observed may change due to the impact that this has on underlying perceptions of scarcity and abundance. As noted earlier, I previously reported some evidence that this may occur (Oliver, 2018). Incidentally, well before the development of

prospect theory, the economist and Nobel Laureate Harry Markowitz (1952) had the insight to see that outcome magnitude may affect responses to risky scenarios, although his theory was also far from complete.

20 In this book, I will not discuss whether the various behavioural phenomena and motivational forces arose from biological or cultural evolution. To me, it is plausible that long-standing cultural practices may have impacted on human biology over time to some degree, and also that biological traits, that became stronger in populations due to natural selection, to some extent influence culture. When I write of evolution, I am simply referring to behavioural phenomena that have emerged, presumably for good reasons, over eons, because they serve humans well in the pursuit of their multifarious desires.

21 There are also circumstances where one may focus excessively on one's own interests which, while not exactly fraudulent, are calculated and will impose harms on others. Indeed, this type of action is perhaps the principal form of harm considered in this book (particularly in Chapter 9).

22 Hume suggested that most people will temper their egoistic instincts, due to a recognition of the wider harms that these can cause. He wrote,

> as it is evident, that every man loves himself better than any other person, he is naturally impelled to extend his acquisitions as much as possible; and nothing can restrain him in this propensity, but reflection and experience, by which he learns the pernicious effects of that licence, and the total dissolution of society which must ensue from it. His original inclination, therefore, or instinct, is here checked and restrained by a subsequent judgment or observation.
>
> *(Hume, 1777/2018, p.218)*

This statement implies that Hume believed that long-term self-interest is learned during one's lifetime, which may at first glance be somewhat at odds with the contention that a tendency towards acting reciprocally has developed organically over eons. However, he may have retorted if he were able, that it is the ability to learn to act reciprocally that is now more or less innate in humans. Putting this minor entanglement aside, the laws, magistrates and judges that he believed are necessary to protect society act as safeguards against those who would otherwise fail to check their egoistic instincts.

23 von Mises disparaged Mill's later views, which he believed were influenced too much by Mill's wife Harriet, for being socialistic.

24 That the influence of the behavioural phenomena can cause inaction that results in others forgoing benefits will also be considered.

CHAPTER 2

1 Of course, Mill did not restrict himself to behavioural public policy, or any precursor to it.

2 For instance, with respect to the third duty, public health care and education systems. Incidentally, if one is searching for political support for the sentiments expressed by Smith and Mill, then one could do worse than the words of one of the great statesmen, Thomas Jefferson, who in his first inaugural address said that 'a wise and frugal government, which shall restrain men from injuring one another, shall leave them otherwise free to regulate their own pursuits of industry and improvement' (for the full address, see https://avalon.law.yale.edu/19th_century/jefinau1.asp).

3 I leave to one side here the important consideration of third-party externalities, which can occur from a process of free and fair exchange and thus in such cases fall beyond the remit of behavioural public policy. I will return to this issue in Chapter 9 also.

4 This might include the regulation of behaviours so that people impose less harms on themselves, or the regulation of those who would otherwise harm others. The latter is presumably a proposition that most non-libertarians would find difficult to contest.

5 Although I reviewed some of these approaches, and illustrated them with interventions proposed by the UK Behavioural Insights Team, in the *Origins* book (Oliver, 2017), it is necessary to discuss them again here to provide clarity on how my preferred framework differs.

6 To pre-empt the discussion that follows, libertarian paternalists actually claim that those targeted for behaviour change are the best deliberative judges of what is good for themselves but often fail to behave accordingly, and thus need some help.

7 Not all behavioural economists are behavioural welfare economists, with Sugden and me being cases in point.

8 Interested readers might consult Camerer and Loewenstein (2003) for a reflection on the development of behavioural economics, Thaler (2015) for

an entertaining, if somewhat American-centric, history of the field, and/or
my *Origins* book for a discussion of the development of behavioural public
policy more generally (Oliver, 2017).

9 In technical jargon, that just described is an example of asymmetric
dominance. Incidentally, arguably the first reported empirical
observations in behavioural economics – the so-called Allais paradoxes –
are violations of the independence axiom (Allais, 1953).

10 Not all decisions that conflict with (at least the caricature of) rational
choice theory are necessarily relatively "quick", however. For instance,
actions and behaviours that have a cooperative intent may be undertaken
after a period of quite intense reflection.

11 There is often a tendency to equate the word "nudging" to the whole of
behavioural public policy, but as we shall see, the former is just one of
many possible frameworks encompassed by the latter.

12 That it is invariably difficult to separate internalities from externalities
has been recognised for a long time. For instance, Berlin (1969, p.xxiv)
wrote 'that anything a man does could, in principle, frustrate others; that
no man is an island; that the social and individual aspects of human beings
often cannot, in practice, be disentangled'. In a similar vein, the economist
Julian Le Grand, with his co-author Bill New, notes that

> if there are very few areas of life that in no way impinge on others'
> consciousness, then presumably there are very few private activities
> that do not lend themselves to intervention on the grounds of a
> psychic cost, even where this cost is not generated by someone
> else's suffering. So, for example, a certain type of sexual practice
> between consenting adults in private, which a segment of the
> population finds morally reprehensible (and the rest of the
> population do not care about one way or another), could be outlawed
> simply with reference to a judgment that the disutility experienced
> by disapproving "onlookers" exceeded the utility of practitioners.
>
> *(Le Grand and New, 2015, p.63)*

Some of the many problems associated with adopting utility maximisation
as the normative goal of public policy will be explored in Chapter 4.

13 Libertarian paternalists contend that because any type of policy setting
includes a form of choice architecture, even if it is not consciously
designed, it is better that it be built so that it is more likely to induce

choices and behaviours that more closely match the deliberative preferences of the targeted population than if the design of the choice architecture were left to accident or bureaucratic process. However, it is debatable that deliberative preferences can be elicited with any degree of accuracy (see Sugden, 2009 and Rizzo and Whitman, 2020). Moreover, given that people have multifarious and differing desires in life, manipulating people in the direction of one overarching goal will almost inevitably conflict with the personal desires of a great many people. It is the contention in this book that public policy makers resist such systematic manipulative tactics and instead focus upon explicit education and information dissemination, supported by open regulation *against* those who use such acts of manipulation that impose substantive harms on others.

14 Loss aversion could be potentially further strengthened in this case if the deposit is not only merely not returned if one fails to meet one's targets, but is donated to what might be considered a particularly obnoxious cause.

15 Sunstein (2020) has recently implied that nudges do not necessarily have to be informed by behavioural science, and has elsewhere labelled as "educative nudges" such instruments as warnings, labels and disclosure statements (Sunstein, 2016). But with no behavioural science input, these are, to me, excluded from the armoury of behavioural public policy. Any behavioural public policy intervention – nudge or otherwise – has to be in some way informed by behavioural science.

16 It is debatable as to whether people can be actively paternalistic towards themselves, but there has been some discussion of the concept of "self-nudging" (e.g. see Reijula and Hertwig, 2022). If people enrol under their own volition in commitment contracts, or if, for example, they place their store of chocolate in a hard-to-reach place (or even refrain from buying chocolate at all), then one might reasonably conclude that interventions that have been loosely labelled as self-nudges are consistent with a liberal framework, given that people autonomously decide to do these things to themselves.

17 Sunstein (2019b) states that '[m]any efforts to increase navigability, embodying a form of means paternalism, retain freedom of choice, and so can be seen as compatible with Mill's harm principle'. I am less convinced that Mill would have found what are, in many instances, behaviourally informed manipulations targeted at internalities,

acceptable, even if people are not, in theory, compelled to adopt particular behaviours or actions.

18 See the work of finance expert Riccardo Rebonato (2012) for a view that governments may use autonomy-undermining libertarian paternalistic interventions for malign purposes (although, strictly speaking, one could argue that interventions that are intentionally malign are not paternalistic).

19 Chapter 4 includes further reflection on the issue of whether some form of predefined aggregate welfare or utility ought to guide policy action.

20 If people were taught about the behavioural influences, they may be more ready to "nudge" themselves against certain impulses. For instance, if a person was made aware of the phenomenon of present bias, he might decide to send his angry emails only to himself and wait a day or so before sending them (or not) to the intended recipient. As suggested in note 16, those who generally oppose libertarian paternalism are likely to be less critical of the notion that people nudge themselves. For an extended discussion on the likelihood that people may often "de-bias" (or self-regulate) themselves against the behavioural influences, see Rizzo and Whitman (2020, pp.218–233).

21 Incidentally, soft paternalism is sometimes defined as an approach that targets only children and the mentally compromised for paternalistic intervention. However, in this book, soft paternalism refers to approaches that purport to retain respect for individual autonomy.

22 Conly is opposed to bans on alcohol consumption on the grounds that as a social lubricant, its benefits are likely to outweigh its costs in many cultures. This gives the impression that coercive paternalists in the behavioural public policy field are searching for justifications to heavily regulate behaviours that they personally dislike. If so, this framework more closely aligns with ends rather than means paternalism.

23 One could claim that the mandated use of seatbelts and motorcycle helmets are shoves, if the reluctance to wear them if regulations are not in place is a consequence of, say, present bias or overconfidence, and if the justification for these interventions is focused entirely on protecting those targeted. At face value, it is difficult (for me) to oppose these laws, particularly if the seatbelt or helmet wearer does not sacrifice much benefit due to these legal requirements. However, those who follow the liberal tradition would conclude that no-one is in a position to make this

judgement other than those who are affected by these laws, which is a view to which I am sympathetic. Thus, beyond educating people on the benefits of wearing seatbelts and helmets – and, to reiterate, so long as not wearing seatbelts or helmets bears no substantive consequences for others – the liberal tradition that I support would leave their wearing to the discretion of the individual.

24 Those lacking agency might include children and those who are not of sound mind, although, admittedly, the age at which a child becomes an adult, and the point at which a mental incapacity is deemed a fundamental challenge to full agency, are both grey areas. Mentally ill behaviours, in the words of the political philosopher Joel Feinberg (1970), tend to be "not interested" – i.e. they serve neither the interests of the person doing them nor anyone else's interests either. Feinberg noted, however, that: 'By no means all mentally ill persons ... suffer from defects of reason. Many or most of them suffer from emotional or volitional disorders that leave their cognitive faculties quite unimpaired. To impose compulsory therapy on such persons would be as objectionably paternalistic as imposing involuntary cures for warts or headaches or tooth decay' (1970, p.279). Presumably, for these people an anti-paternalist would not limit his aversion to compulsion and manipulation to therapy alone.

25 Strictly speaking, libertarian paternalism does not require people to be nudged in the direction of utility maximisation – it merely requires people to be nudged in the direction that they deliberatively say that they want to go (Thaler and Sunstein, 2008). But behavioural welfare economists, including Thaler (2015) himself, hold on to utility maximisation as the normative ideal and most of the paternalistic behavioural public policy frameworks reviewed in this chapter appear to accept this postulate.

26 Budges form the second arm of the political economy of behavioural public policy proposed in this book. The first arm – to try to ensure that the general characteristics of society crowd in, and do not crowd out, the deep inclination for people to reciprocate with each other – is not an intervention "type" that can be placed along the dimensions of the behavioural public policy cube. Although it is behavioural-informed in that it recognises the importance of reciprocity as a human motivation, the approach supports open education and information dissemination. And although it calls for a great deal of individual autonomy as conducive to people benefiting themselves *and* others, facilitating cooperative

tendencies is also likely to require regulatory intervention, as will be discussed in Chapter 5.

27 Admittedly, as intimated in note 23, some anti-paternalists will feel uncomfortable with any attempt to identify what is a small cost to another person; they will contend that the only person who can determine the cost of an action to any particular person is that person himself. I am one of those anti-paternalists. That aside, some advocates of nudging have an unfortunate habit of referring only to the most innocuous of interventions when defending their approach at a general level.

CHAPTER 3

1 If having paternalists in government is unavoidable, I personally would want them to be in the Gus O'Donnell mould.

2 In principle, any actor can act paternalistically towards any other actor, but here I am principally concerned with paternalistic actions by the state.

3 The political theorist Albert Weale, in commenting on why we should value freedom, similarly notes that:

> One such reason is that individual liberty enables a person to carry through his "plan of life", that is, to pursue the various ends to which he has committed himself in their interrelationship to each other. Individual liberty is important because it provides the necessary context in which a person may pursue his ends in ways which match his own conception of himself as a person. Therefore, to deny someone this individual liberty, by making him do something which is inconsistent with his own freely chosen life plan, is to alienate a person from himself, since it is to alienate him from the ends to which he has committed himself.
>
> *(Weale, 1978, p.170)*

Incidentally, distinctions between autonomy and freedom are made in the literature. For example, as aforementioned, Le Grand and New (2015) contend that autonomy is the ability to act as deliberating agents, which can be undermined even if freedom – i.e. the absence of physical constraints over what one might choose – remains untouched (thus, in relation to the discussion in Chapter 2, it is possible that some nudge interventions preserve freedom on these terms but impact negatively on autonomy). Although these semantic distinctions may be important in the context of other discussions, they are not a major concern in this book. Here, autonomy, freedom and liberty are taken as interchangeable terms.

4 Admittedly, paternalists tend to view many beings as irrational (or at least biased), thus justifying their interference in individual behaviours. As an aside, Kant saw things, including people, as having two possible sources of value, which are their usefulness towards achieving other ends, and their intrinsic value – i.e. as an end in themselves. In Kant's theory, people must reach an agreement on how we all must treat one another, and thus there is a heavy emphasis on mutual respect. The philosopher Elizabeth Anderson (1993) sees value as many more sided than this. For example, she argues that inanimate nature – ecosystems – cannot be respected in the Kantian sense because inanimate nature cannot enter into reciprocal relations that are based on a conscious acceptance of common principles, yet nature is not just valued for its usefulness either. Anderson thus defines an important component of the value for nature as "appreciation".

5 A failure to benefit harms by denying positive externalities, as opposed to imposing negative externalities.

6 Note that although Mill believed that it is legitimate to regulate against harms, he did not believe that all negative externalities are unallowable.

7 The first part of the above quotation demonstrates Mill's concern that preventing people from thinking for themselves may erode their ability to think deliberatively, which, as noted in Chapter 2, is a worry shared by those who developed the think, nudge-plus, boost and budge approaches.

8 Although this might not be the case for all anti-paternalists. For instance, the covert nature of some forms of soft paternalism might legitimately be viewed as highly statist by some anti-paternalists, who may therefore prefer explicit forms of hard paternalism that can be more openly considered and challenged.

9 One could make the philosophical argument that if we have only a fairly tenuous connection to our future self, then that future self might better be thought of as a different person. If so, then interventions intended to protect our future self from our current self are perhaps aimed at addressing an externality rather than being paternalistically driven. A different externality-related point can be made if we recognise that the most significant future harm generated by people who save little for their retirements now might not be imposed on their future selves, but rather on the future young, who may be required to cross-transfer far more resources than they otherwise

would in order to support their parents and grandparents. But for the purposes of this chapter, we will follow the convention that efforts to increase retirement savings are acts of paternalism.

10 Arguments that refer to limited imagination or limited foresight to justify paternalistic interventions contend that one's older self would have known better – that it is one's younger self that makes mistakes. However, it may be the case that one's older self has, to a degree, forgotten the desires and fulfilment that one's younger self experienced from the decisions that were made years, even decades, ago. That is, the failure of imagination, if it exists, may work in both temporal directions. If so, perhaps the decisions that one's younger self made were not obvious mistakes after all.

11 An exception might be where the *anticipated* regret in addition to the realised regret is larger than the positive welfare effect of the person's uncoerced behaviours. In this case, we may be sure that coercion, by removing the anticipated and realised regret (and if the intervention stirs no other negative feelings), will increase the person's welfare.

12 Incidentally, succumbing to temptations may enrich a life. Adam and Eve may have lived in somewhat stupefying happiness if Eve had not been tempted by the fruit of knowledge, but who is to say that most of us would not deliberatively prefer to eat that fruit, even when well aware of the misery that knowledge may bring. As Mill (1863/1969, p.121) famously wrote in *Utilitarianism*:

> It is indisputable that the being whose capacities of enjoyment are low, has the greatest chance of having them fully satisfied; and a highly endowed being will always feel that any happiness which he can look for, as the world is constituted, is imperfect. But he can learn to bear its imperfections, if they are at all bearable; and they will not make him envy the being who is indeed unconscious of the imperfections, but only because he feels not at all the good which those imperfections qualify. It is better to be a human being dissatisfied than a pig satisfied; better to be Socrates dissatisfied than a fool satisfied. And if the fool, or the pig, is of a different opinion, it is only because they only know their own side of the question.

Admittedly, succumbing to the temptation of too many doughnuts, for example, may not offer as much benefit as the fruit of knowledge, but consuming a relatively large amount of the former may, for many, still enrich their lives in some sense.

13 In this quote, Le Grand and New are not limiting themselves to behavioural public policy, but the argument applies to the relevant issues in behavioural public policy also. On indirect paternalism, which Dworkin (1972) calls impure paternalism, see also Feinberg (1986).

14 They illustrate their point with a true story of a stuntman who took a film production company to a tribunal after a stunt that he had performed had gone wrong. The stuntman claimed that he had been reluctant to perform the stunt but was coerced into doing so by the company. He claimed that, because of the company's actions, he was not thinking straight when making his decision and thus had not given voluntary consent to performing the stunt. Thus, according to the stuntman, the company, and not he himself, had harmed him (see Le Grand and New, 2015, pp.114–115).

15 Sunstein (2019a, pp.11–12) sees even the weather as a form of choice architecture: 'On snowy days, for example, people are especially likely to purchase cars with four wheel drive, which they do not always love.' If we define choice architecture in a general sense, then Sunstein is of course right – it is always there. But if, as also noted in Chapter 2, we consider it in the sense of it being used, often covertly, by one actor to guide specifically the behaviours of another actor that align with the first actor's intended directions, then it can be problematic. Private actors do this all the time, but if they overstep the mark, their actions can be regulated. Many feel uncomfortable with public policy actors using similar tactics, particularly in relation to paternalistic interventions, since it challenges government accountability.

16 The argument here is that nobody (including policy makers) can definitively judge that another person is making errors in how they are living their lives according to their own preferences to the extent that we manipulate or coerce that person to make different decisions, if their actions impose no harms on others. Attempts can be made to educate them, but ultimately even a seemingly well-defined concept such as present bias may not be a bias at all – people exhibiting this affect may just prefer to live in the moment. Of course, libertarian paternalists maintain that nudges allow people the liberty to do just that if they so wish – and thus Sunstein (2019b), for instance, sees libertarian paternalism as a

Millian approach – but, as noted in Chapter 2, there are legitimate concerns that liberty may not be preserved with what are essentially covert interventions.

17 This statement is perhaps more consistent with the think and nudge-plus approaches (and also perhaps the boost approach, although, as noted in Chapter 2, boosts are more closely aligned with open education than paternalism) than with the nudge approach because nudges, in attempting to alter people's automatic (i.e. unthinking) choices and behaviours, may indeed affect the "real them".

18 See Anderson (2017), for example, for a discussion that touches upon the differences between classical liberalism and neoliberalism (and neoclassical economics).

19 The so-called neoliberal political platforms of Margaret Thatcher and Ronald Reagan perhaps further muddied this picture, not least because Hayek was one of Thatcher's intellectual heroes. Moreover, that Americans tend to describe those who support heavy state intervention as liberals confuses matters further still (and is possibly a hangover from a time when liberalism was associated with egalitarianism – see Anderson, 2017), but behavioural public policy is confusing enough, so I will leave these points hanging.

20 Von Mises and Hayek were in part reacting against what they saw as the rise of authoritarianism – specifically for them, strands of socialism and communism – in the times in which they lived, internationally and in and close to the country of their birth. It is important to remind people of the value of freedom when authoritarianism is on the rise. Incidentally, one should, however, perhaps be somewhat circumspect of von Mises's predictive powers. For instance, although later to seek exile in New York himself, in 1927 he wrote that 'the deeds of the Fascists and of other parties corresponding to them were emotional reflex actions evoked by indignation of the deeds of the Bolsheviks and Communists. As soon as the first flush of anger had passed, their policy took a more moderate course and will probably become even more so with the passage of time' (von Mises, 1927/2005, p.28).

21 See Sunstein (2022) for an attempt at introducing a Hayekian behavioural economics, and Rizzo and Whitman (2022) and Sugden (2022) for critiques of that attempt.

22 If a convincing argument for intervening was offered on externality grounds, then that would of course be a different story. Even with

externality arguments, however, there are alternatives to mandating, say, the use of motorcycle helmets. For example, if the externality consideration focuses upon the additional costs of public health care treatment for those who do not wear a helmet (compared to those that do) when suffering an accident, then a regulation could be introduced that requires such persons to pay a surcharge for their consequent medical care.

CHAPTER 4

1 Although, as we shall see, many scholars at various times did not equate the whole of utility with our own individual happiness (or pleasure). Also, standard economic theory only requires preferences (or, rather, choices) to be consistent – it does not prescribe what will or ought to comprise a person's utility. I will come on to this later in the chapter.

2 However, it has to be admitted that Hume, great thinker and writer though he was, did not lack entirely the capacity to confuse. For instance, elsewhere, he pre-empted Bentham by stating that pleasure and the avoidance of pain are the ultimate ends:

> Ask a man *why he uses exercise;* he will answer *because he desires to keep his health.* If you then enquire, *why he desires health,* he will reply, *because sickness is painful.* If you push your enquiries farther, and desire a reason *why he hates pain,* it is impossible he can ever give any. This is the ultimate end, and is never referred to any other object. Perhaps to your second question, why he desires health, he may also reply, that it is necessary for the exercise of his calling. If you ask, why he is anxious on that head, he will answer, because he desires to get money. If you demand Why? It is the instrument of pleasure, says he. And beyond this it is an absurdity to ask for a reason.
>
> *(Hume, 1751/2018, pp.93–94)*

To be fair to Hume, he may have meant that individual (personal) utility is focused on pleasure whereas social utility has to incorporate broader considerations (although he did contend that prosocial actions are driven by personal self-interest), or he may have meant that action and indolence also ultimately reduce to pleasure (although, in which case, why would he separate them into different components?). Whatever drove his reasoning, it is not self-evident that pleasure and the avoidance of pain (or indeed utility or happiness) are the ultimate ends for all human beings; they are only the ultimate ends (for you) if you believe them to be so. In an *Imagine* programme for the BBC reflecting back on her life, the Nobel Prize-winning novelist Toni Morrison balked at the idea that happiness was the ultimate end, and suggested that people – perhaps like Eve – fundamentally sought wisdom. For some this may be true, but to me it is also too prescriptive. I will later contend that people have a multitude of desires that vary across individuals (and indeed within individuals across contexts), and that desires precede (and are not *always* associated with) any felt utility, rather than necessarily being driven by the expectation of experiencing utility.

3 The economist Douglas Bernheim (2010) has suggested that what might appear to be adaptation to one's circumstances from some form of self-reported assessment might be due to differences in the psychological calibration of the reporting scale, rather than people genuinely feeling that an objectively worse state is no worse than a formerly better state (the same argument applies when a person appears to adapt to an improvement in his circumstances, which has possible implications for the so-called Easterlin paradox – e.g. see Easterlin, 1974). For example, a slave may be internally less happy than a free man, but if people differentially normalise the happiness reporting scale based on their experiences and expectations, then that objective internal difference in happiness may not be reflected in a difference in reported happiness. Sen (1985) makes a similar point when stating that the impoverished may learn to live with realistic desires and thus gain pleasure from small mercies.

4 Embedded within utilitarianism is the assumption that people have a declining marginal utility of income/money/wealth. That is, an additional £100 gives more utility (pleasure) on average to a person who earns £10,000 per annum than if he earned £50,000 per annum, and gives more utility in the latter position than if he earned £500,000 per annum, etc. Therefore, on the general subject of inequality, if it is assumed that everyone has the same marginal utility of income curve then utility would be maximised if everyone had the same income. But that is a strong assumption.

5 There is likely to be more support for the consequentialist claim if the individuals differ more markedly in age – for instance, a 15-year-old versus an 85-year-old. However, there are of course many ways in which utilitarianism might be viewed as problematic. For instance, as noted in

note 12 in Chapter 2 (and also with respect to rights), if the aggregate disutility of those who (merely) disapprove of a certain sexual practice outweighs the utility of those who (actively) engage in and support that practice, then the practice would be outlawed if the basic utilitarian calculus is followed (although, admittedly, such practices may be difficult to monitor).

6 There is a lot of literature on the capability approach, with scholars other than Sen contributing to its development, most notably the philosopher Martha Nussbaum. See, for example, Nussbaum (2013).

7 Mill's version of utilitarianism resonates with Hume's writings in that he maintained that his ideas were informed by the golden rule of the New Testament (i.e. do unto others as you would have them do unto you – a call for reciprocity). Although I also support using the golden rule to inform public policy design, I do so without reference to the interpersonal trade-off of utility (see my *Reciprocity* book).

8 Pareto efficiency is, in itself, silent on the issue of distribution.

9 The mathematician John von Neumann and the economist Oskar Morgenstern worked together at Princeton University during the Second World War. The axioms of expected utility theory form a very small part of their *Theory of Games and Economic Behavior*, and yet are among the most important developments in the history of economic thought. For more detail on the axioms (principally, ordering, transitivity, continuity and independence) and the development of the theory, see my *Origins* book.

10 There is a theoretically identical alternative method to the certainty equivalence method called the probability equivalence method. With the latter, in an example analogous to the one just given, an individual is informed that he could accept, say, £50 for certain or a gamble that offers a probability, p, of winning £100 but that also has a 1-p chance of winning nothing. The individual is then asked for the p required for him to be indifferent between the guaranteed outcome and the gamble. If he states that he would require a 60 per cent chance of a positive payoff from the gamble, then again normalising the utilities of £0 and £100 at 0 and 1, respectively, the utility of £50 for this individual is $0.6*1 + 0.4*0 = 0.6$. In health policy, for instance, the outcomes do not have to be money – they can be states of health, with the endpoints defined as immediate death and full health for a statistical lifetime. Indeed, in health economic evaluation, the probability equivalence method is one of the ways in which units of

benefit called quality adjusted life-years, or QALYs, are typically in large part derived. In that context, the probability equivalence method is called the standard gamble, and QALYs are used to help inform practical health care priority-setting decisions.

11 See, for example, my *Reciprocity* book.

12 Since behavioural economics grew principally from a critique of the descriptive (not the normative) validity of vNM expected utility theory, we can perhaps assume that the utility that behavioural welfare economists implicitly adhere to is of the hedonic kind (or at least of the egoistic kind). Note as an aside that technical behavioural economists have made several attempts over the years to generalise expected utility theory by weakening the axiomatic requirements so that it captures a wider set of preferences, including at least some of those that violate standard rational choice theory. However, these models still require consistency with a number of axioms, and still assume that people seek to maximise some conception of utility. Few of those models have had much influence.

13 Rizzo and Whitman (2020), drawing on the work of Gigerenzer, refer to the vNM postulates as "puppet" rationality, and advocate for consideration of a more inclusive rationality in which people adopt reasonable strategies that may conflict with the assumptions of standard theory in order to navigate the real world. They thus also contend that violations of the vNM axioms are not necessarily caused by biases or errors.

14 Implicitly in relation to the different definitions of utility, the cognitive psychologist Steven Pinker writes (NB. Pinker's use of the word "happy" corresponds to my use of the word "pleasure"):

> People who lead happy but not necessarily meaningful lives have all their needs satisfied: they are healthy, have enough money, and feel good a lot of the time. People who lead meaningful lives may enjoy none of these boons. Happy people live in the present; those with meaningful lives have a narrative about their past and a plan for the future. Those with happy but meaningless lives are takers and beneficiaries; those with meaningful but unhappy lives are givers and benefactors. Parents get meaning from their children, but not necessarily happiness. Time spent with friends makes a life happier; time spent with loved ones makes it more meaningful. Stress, worry, arguments, challenges, and struggles make a life unhappier but more meaningful. It's not that people with meaningful lives

masochistically go looking for trouble but that meaning is about expressing rather than satisfying the self: it is enhanced by activities that define the person and build a reputation.

(Pinker, 2018, p.267)

15 For example, see work undertaken by the economists Dan Benjamin (and his colleagues) and John Helliwell (Benjamin *et al.*, 2020; Helliwell, 2020).

16 When reflecting on similar issues, Hume (1751/2018, p.93) drew on an analogy of how a pillar is constructed. 'Attend to Palladio and Perrault', he wrote,

> while they explain all the parts and proportions of a pillar. They talk of the cornice, and frieze, and base, and entablature, and shaft, and architrave; and give the description and position of each of these members. But should you ask the description and position of its beauty, they would readily reply, that the beauty is not in any of the parts or members of a pillar, but results from the whole, when that complicated figure is presented to an intelligent mind, susceptible to those finer sensations.

17 Some economists may maintain that the preferred shape(s) of a utility profile, as a part of utility that might be related to, for example, the sense of fulfilment or meaning that a person gets out of an experience, is just an additional argument that can be added to the utility function. One gets the sense that whenever economists (and others) who adopt this perspective hit a bump in their theoretical road, their stock response is to widen the utility function. But then, going back to Berlin (1969), such a widening risks vacuity.

18 As mentioned briefly in Chapter 2, Hertwig (2017) makes a similar argument in relation to the normative underpinning of welfare economics and the consequent justification for using boosts rather than nudges.

19 Hayek's concerns about measuring welfare on a single scale resonate with his similar concerns regarding a planned economy. He wrote that:

> Economic control is not merely control of a sector of human life which can be separated from the rest; it is the control of the means for all our ends. And whoever has sole control of the means must also determine which ends are to be served, which values are to be rated higher and which lower, in short, what men should believe and strive for. Central planning means that the economic problem is to be solved

by the community instead of by the individual; but this involves that
it must also be the community, or rather its representatives, who
must decide the relative importance of the different needs.

(Hayek, 1944/2001, p.95)

Hayek (p.100) goes on to argue that since the planner cannot take into
account the likes and dislikes of different individuals, he uses abstractions
such as "social welfare" and the "good of the community" to justify his
actions; legitimising policy action by appealing to aggregate utility is a
form of central planning.

20 This conjecture may resonate with Anderson's pluralist theory of value
(implicitly referred to in Chapter 3). Anderson (1993, pp.14–15) states that:
'The pluralism of ideals and the relational character of importance also
imply that the ways one person should value a particular thing or person
need not be the ways another person should value it or him.' She contends
that welfarism, by imposing a monistic and reductionist theory of value,
unacceptably bypasses this variety. Given the complexity of value, it may
often be difficult, perhaps impossible, for people to even articulate why
they desire particular things.

21 Although Sugden used the term "the view from nowhere" pejoratively, he
borrowed the phrase from the philosopher Thomas Nagel (1986), who
believed utility maximisation to be an appropriate position to take in moral
reasoning. As is clear, my sympathies lie with Sugden in that I maintain
that the definition of utility is confused and confusing, and that – whatever
its definition – to assume that it drives and ought to drive all human action
is not consistent with what many people do or want to do. It is thus the
pejorative sense that served as the motivation for the title of this chapter.

22 The political scientist James March (1974, p.134) wrote that: 'It seems to
me perfectly obvious that a description that assumes goals come first and
action comes later is frequently radically wrong.'

23 Cf. once again the work of, for example, Nussbaum and Sen on the
capability approach.

24 So long as, as I shall argue in Chapter 9, they are not substantively
harming others.

25 The classical utilitarian framework, in common with the frameworks that
have dominated behavioural public policy to date, lends itself to
arguments for paternalistic intervention from a supposedly benign social
planner. Standard economists tend to be opposed to such acts of social

engineering, as indeed are liberal economists, at least in relation to the economist's own role. For example, James Buchanan (1979) explicitly wrote that economists should not be social engineers, and should limit themselves to offering advice on which institutions might best facilitate people in the pursuit of their various possible desires.

26 See Chater (2022) for a recent discussion of why choice inconsistencies are not necessarily a cause for concern. Bernheim (2010) offers a normative welfarist framework that can, he maintains, accommodate the choice inconsistencies.

CHAPTER 5

1 As I have suggested earlier in this book, paternalistic arguments that it is legitimate to allow policy makers to shape the choice architecture so that people are guided in directions that the policy maker sees fit should be treated with some scepticism.

2 It may sound a little odd to say that a person who has achieved a desire to do nothing with his life – or has renounced ambition and has lived his life by that doctrine – has flourished. It may also appear strange that Russell's masochist (see Chapter 4), in having inflicted pain upon himself, has flourished. That is, some people's desires may seem, to others, the antithesis of what it means to flourish. But I maintain here that both of those individuals (i.e. the inert person and the masochist), in having done what they desired to do, have, on their own terms, flourished, irrespective of what a third person with different desires might think.

3 Mill's tree analogy is the inspiration for the cover of this book. Incidentally, Berlin, in his introduction to *On Liberty*, commented that:

> For [Mill] man differs from animals primarily neither as the possessor of reason, nor as an inventor of tools and methods, but as a being capable of choice, one who is most himself in choosing and not being chosen for; the rider and not the horse; the seeker of ends, and not merely of means, ends that he pursues, each in his own fashion: with the corollary that the more various these fashions, the richer the lives of men become.
>
> *(Berlin, 1969, p.xi)*

4 There are important differences between liberals in relation to many aspects of economic theory. For example, the founder of the Austrian School, Carl

Menger, believed that consumer valuations and incomes play a significant role in determining the prices of goods, in contrast to Smith's contention that price is largely determined by the cost of production (see, for example, the economic historian Bruce Caldwell's biography of Hayek – Caldwell, 2005, pp.17–38). But they all placed a high premium on liberty.

5 Buchanan (1979, p.152) wrote that an individual is a better judge of his own 'better-offness' than any external observer.

6 Darwin did not mean to imply that fitness necessarily equates to physical fitness; rather, he intended fitness to indicate that which is best suited to its environment.

7 Smith's friend David Hume (1751/2018) expressed a similar view in his *An Enquiry Concerning the Principles of Morals*. As noted, Smith actually expressed the view that negative reciprocity – i.e. the threat of punishment for transgressions – is the most important aspect of reciprocity in holding societies together, and negative reciprocity, even of a deliberative as opposed to a more instinctively attitudinal kind, may have strong evolutionary roots. For instance, in *The Descent of Man*, Darwin (1879/2004, p.90) wrote that:

> Sir Andrew Smith, a zoologist whose scrupulous accuracy was known to many persons, told me the following story of which he was himself an eye-witness; at the Cape of Good Hope an officer had often plagued a certain baboon, and the animal, seeing him approaching on Sunday for parade, poured water into a hole and hastily made some thick mud, which he skilfully dashed over the officer as he passed by, to the amusement of many bystanders. For long afterwards the baboon rejoiced and triumphed whenever he saw his victim.

8 On this point, Friedman and Friedman (1980/1990, p.27) wrote that:

> Narrow preoccupation with the economic market has led to a narrow interpretation of self-interest as myopic selfishness, as exclusive concern with immediate material rewards. Economics has been berated for allegedly drawing far-reaching conclusions from a wholly unrealistic "economic man" who is little more than a calculating machine, responding only to monetary stimuli. That is a great mistake. Self-interest is not myopic selfishness. It is whatever it is that interests the participants, whatever they value, whatever goals they pursue. The scientist seeking to advance the frontiers of

his discipline, the missionary seeking to convert infidels to the true faith, the philanthropist seeking to bring comfort to the needy – all are pursuing their interests, as they see them, as they judge them by their own values.

9 Unlike the neoliberals, de Tocqueville did not celebrate selfishness.

10 Anderson (2017), suggests that an egalitarian vision for liberalism was most prominently in focus in the years between Adam Smith and Thomas Paine, and Abraham Lincoln. Perhaps more so for Europeans, the vision outlived Lincoln.

11 It is perhaps worth noting that Marxists argue that the division of labour separates men and women from the intrinsic value of their work – that they cannot feel a close relationship with the fruits of their labour when producing repetitive components (e.g. with a steering wheel or an exhaust pipe, as opposed to a whole car). There is some merit in that argument, but perhaps most people only work to secure money to support their real desires in life. If people have an intrinsic motivation to build a whole car, they can still do that in their leisure time.

12 To reiterate from Chapter 1, and as discussed in some depth in my *Reciprocity* book, there are of course many possible negative consequences of reciprocal actions, in both their positive and negative forms, including its capacity to breed cronyism, fundamentalism, nationalism, resentment, retaliation, retribution, and the like.

13 Whether one wants to believe that people's choices are driven by the expectation of some concept of utility (as appears to be the assumption that many classical liberals held), or whether people just act on desires with utility perhaps, but not necessarily, being a consequence of those desires, the potential to benefit (whether via utility maximisation or the opportunity to flourish as I have defined it) is aided by cooperative, reciprocal – as opposed to selfishly egoistical – actions.

14 In modern-day America, many might contend that egoism – together with mutual suspicion and contempt – has triumphed. The impression that is often given is of an increasingly divided nation, a picture that is applicable to many other countries also. However, at the community level across much of the United States (and elsewhere) the spirit of reciprocity and cooperation is still likely to be very much alive. The tendency to reciprocate can be (and probably in many contexts has been) crowded out unless one is careful, but the point is that this tendency, even if dormant,

still lies within people, and can be revived. Buchanan (1979) made a similar point when he noted that the institutional constraints within which man acts have developed over time in part by accident, in part by evolutionary process, in part by technological necessity and in part by (correctly and incorrectly conceived) constructive design. He maintained that institutions have been allowed to develop that exacerbate the temptation to act egoistically, and that they thus need to be modified to be consistent with man's capacity to be a genuine social animal.

15 Rosenblatt (2018) points out that the school of thought adopted by some French liberals who in the late nineteenth century advocated reductions in income and wealth inequality so as to strengthen social cohesion is called solidarism or liberal socialism. One suspects that the members of the Austrian School would have viewed this, probably disdainfully, as firmly placed in the socialist rather than the liberal camp, but the liberal socialists' emphasis, like the Austrians, was on promoting and protecting freedom. Thus, there appears to be a consensus on (freedom as an) ends, if not always the means.

16 To pre-empt Chapter 6, many people are likely to believe that chief executive officers are *undeserving* of these massive increases in their relative pay.

17 I am assuming that the extent to which one can pursue one's own desires is an indication of how free one is, and that one is more likely to go further in the pursuit of those desires if reciprocity and cooperation are widespread.

18 In relation to the importance of localised decision-making, de Tocqueville (1835/1998, pp.211–212) wrote that:

> The legislators of America ... thought that it would be well to infuse political life into each portion of the territory in order to multiply to an infinite extent opportunities of acting in concert for all the members of the community and to make them constantly feel their mutual dependence ... if the object be to have the local affairs of a district conducted by the men who reside there, the same persons are always in contact, and they are, in a manner, forced to be acquainted and to adapt themselves to one another .... Local freedom, then, which leads a great number of citizens to value the affection of their neighbours and of their kindred, perpetually brings men together and forces them to help one another in spite of the propensities that sever them.

A little later, Mill (1859/1969, p.104) noted that: 'Speaking generally, there is no one so fit to conduct any business, or to determine how or by whom it shall be conducted, as those who are personally interested in it.' Moreover, Friedman and Friedman (1980/1990, p.157) wrote that:

> In small communities the individual citizen feels that he has, and indeed does have, more control over what the political authorities do than in large communities ... he has a considerable opportunity to affect what happens ... local governments must provide their citizens with services they regard as worth the taxes they pay or either be replaced or suffer a loss of taxpayers.

And Buchanan (1979, p.223) noted that 'the smaller the number of persons with whom a person interacts, the higher the likelihood he will seem to behave in accordance with something akin to the Kantian generalization principle: in our terminology, that he will provide public good in his choice behavior'. As discussed in my *Reciprocity* book, the economist Elinor Ostrom wrote extensively and powerfully on the ability of local actors to tackle collective problems more effectively when unencumbered by central state interferences (e.g. see Ostrom, 1990, 2000).

19 It is of course important that central and local-level decision-makers can work well together; unfortunately, this is not always the case, as witnessed by policy responses to the 2020 coronavirus pandemic in some countries (see, for example: www.cambridge.org/core/journals/health-economics-policy-and-law/hepl-blog-series-covid19-pandemic). Incidentally, de Tocqueville distinguished between the centralisation of government and the centralisation of administration, where government refers to general laws, international relations, etc. and administration refers to specific policy concerns. He wrote that:

> Certain interests are common to all parts of a nation, such as the enactment of general laws and the maintenance of its foreign relations. Other interests are peculiar to certain parts of the nation, such, for instance, as the business of several townships .... I cannot conceive that a nation can live and prosper without a powerful centralisation of government. But I am of the opinion that a centralised administration is fit only to enervate the nations in which it exists, by incessantly diminishing their local spirit.
>
> *(de Tocqueville, 1835/1998, p.41)*

Perhaps modern public sector services are well positioned to benefit from this local spirit, assuming, of course, that local decision-makers are beholden to the interests of the communities they serve.

CHAPTER 6

1 In mentioning Mill's views on desert, it is perhaps noteworthy that pursuing this notion can lead to circumstances unprescribed by consequentialist utilitarian concerns. For instance, a non-deserving person may gain more utility, however defined, from a reward than that gained by a deserving person (although it might be argued that the utility gained by others in society from seeing merit-based justice served rebalances the calculus). Feinberg (1970, p.94) himself commented that: 'Desert is essentially a nonutilitarian concept, one which can and often does come into head-on conflict with utility.' That said, he continued that 'there is no a priori reason for giving [desert] automatic priority over all other values. Desert is one very important kind of ethical consideration, but it is not the only one.' In a partial defence of Mill on this point, he suggests that punishment is particularly deserved if the act that is punished in some way undermines the collective interest, thus harming a whole community (including, perhaps, the transgressor); thus one could make the argument that if the threat of punishment deters such actions it may prevent much unhappiness. Mill would also fold the very notion of a concern for desert and justice into his broad definition of utility, but as touched upon in Chapter 4, there are difficulties associated with doing that.

2 I reviewed some of de Waal's work in my *Reciprocity* book.

3 Hamann et al. (2013) did not observe any merit-based concern among three year-olds who engaged in a similar non-collaborative task, which led the authors to conclude that collaboration is a crucial component in the development of equitable – or merit-based – sharing.

4 Scholars from a range of disciplines have undertaken work on the ultimatum game. See, for example, the work published by the behavioural economists Colin Camerer and Richard Thaler (1995), the evolutionary biologist Joseph Henrich and his colleagues (2005) and the economist Alvin Roth (1995).

5 See, for example, the writings by Camerer (2003), the experimental economists Christoph Engel (2011) and Armin Falk and Urs Fischbacher (2006), and, again, Henrich *et al.* (2005).

6 I have collected data that suggests that if people who assume the role of Player I are required to earn their endowments in the ultimatum game, their offers are substantially lower than those that are typically reported in the literature, and that those who are required to respond are overwhelmingly willing to accept nothing (or next to nothing) when they are aware that the proposers have earned their endowments. See Oliver (2022).

7 Ruffle (1998), in the article aforementioned, also tested the effect of Player II earned endowments on Player I allocations in the dictator game, with results consistent with those reported by Oxoby and Spraggon.

8 People may still cooperate under a cloud of fear, but fear does not sit well with mutually beneficial actions, and without mutual benefit the cooperation is unlikely to be sustained.

9 Public or popular opinion might of course often clamour for greater punishment for a misdemeanour than a deeper reflection on justice (or even common sense) will warrant. Given the complexity and malleability of desert, and the need for criminal justice systems to consider punishment, penitence, reformation, deterrence and the like, it is likely that the scales of justice will often be considered by many to be somewhat unbalanced. To sustain a justice system, or group cohesion, or even personal relationships, it is important to explain clearly the rationale for why a particular punishment is deserved, and then hopefully, over time, a compromise might be reached if there is intractable disagreement pertaining to this explanation. Both sides to the exchange have to be satisfied that the punishment fits the crime – that desert is given its proper due.

10 Much of what follows applies also in relation to reward, but for ease of exposition I will focus on negative reciprocity here.

11 Heinrich (2021) presents evidence that suggests that the extent to which people consider motives when apportioning blame differs across different cultures.

12 In Action type C_2 compared to Action type C_1, the causal relevance condition has been weakened.

13 In the positive domain, Action type C_1 might be that the action is welcome, and Action type C_2 that the action is neutral. For example, if Sir John was so agreeable at the dinner table that he relaxed Lady Mary to such an extent that she later beat everyone at billiards, Sir John might deserve

some credit for her victory. If the same were to occur except that she was not undefeated at billiards, we would have the positive mirror image of Action type D_1: Sir John would deserve no credit for the billiard victory, because the victory did not happen, but his agreeable nature over dinner might still serve as a signal that he is a person with whom one might wish to cooperate/reciprocate in the future.

14 Rawls allows inequality under the assumption that some inequality, as an engine of aspiration and growth, for example, may benefit the worst off.

15 There will also be some who would prefer to refrain from assisting even the deserving poor.

CHAPTER 7

1 Note that in Chapter 6 some evidence was presented that suggests that the propensity to share on the basis of desert in very young children depends on whether a task is undertaken collaboratively or in isolation. With reference to some of the arguments presented in Chapter 5, different levels of productivity cannot account for the increasing concentrations of income and wealth in the hands of a small proportion of the world's population over the past few decades.

2 The economist Erte Xiao and the philosopher Cristina Bicchieri undertook a trust game between hypothetical investors and beneficiaries. They reported that in cases where reciprocation by a beneficiary in response to an initial investment would increase the inequality between the two parties, about 40 per cent of the beneficiaries reciprocated; however, if such action would not widen inequality, 70 per cent of the beneficiaries reciprocated (Xiao and Bicchieri, 2010). From this, the authors concluded that inequality aversion can sometimes trump the motivation to reciprocate.

3 It may often be difficult to demarcate private from public concerns. As intimated by Berlin (1969), many private actions will of course have social consequences and those consequences will be widely believed to fall within the remit of public sector policy. For instance, a person may choose, privately, to eat five doughnuts each day, and in many countries he will have access to public health care treatment if he suffers ill health perhaps as a consequence (an alternative topical example is where the private decision to consume meat can, in the aggregate, have a substantial

environmental impact). Many will take the view that manipulative and/or coercive anti-doughnut-eating public sector interventions are legitimate because they may save those who consume a lot of doughnuts from themselves, but so long as consuming doughnuts is not harming other people I would contend that an individual's doughnut-eating practices are his own private concern (assuming that he is not being substantively manipulated or coerced into eating more doughnuts than he really desires). We can attempt to educate him of the potential harms of his behaviour, but no more than that. If a healthy living life were considered within the realm of manipulative or coercive public policy, then each of us who is able might find ourselves, against our better judgement, living on a diet of steamed vegetables and running for five miles each day, but I suspect that a society that was organised as such would be an unappealing prospect to most.

4 During the pandemic, arguments were made in favour of shielding subsectors of the population, particularly the elderly, on paternalistic grounds, but a liberal would still contend that if external transmission from the infected elderly is not at all a concern, then beyond education, the elderly ought to be left to make their own decisions on how to live their lives. That is, the only legitimate justification to manipulate or limit freedoms remains that pertaining to mitigating negative externalities.

5 If millions of people were eating five doughnuts every day and the consequent link to health care consumption was proven and substantial, there may be a strong argument to regulate against the excessive consumption of doughnuts (or to limit doughnut consumers' access to relevant health care services) on externality grounds, if the health care services that these doughnut consumers use are publicly financed. There is also an argument to regulate the seller of doughnuts if we conclude that he is manipulating the buyer into purchasing more doughnuts than he otherwise would. Such a regulation would be an example of a budge intervention, which will be considered in more depth in Chapter 9.

6 Over time and place, of course, the demarcation of the two domains is often blurred.

7 A possible reason why Adam Smith emphasised the importance of prosocial behaviours in his *Theory of Moral Sentiments* and of self-love in *The Wealth of Nations* is because the former dealt with social relations, and the latter focused on economic transactions.

8 Sellers can attempt to exploit buyers by demanding a price that is too high for the quality of the service or product that they are offering, which may incentivise buyers to go elsewhere. Conversely, in situations where buyers are not price-takers, sellers can try to secure other buyers of their products or services if they feel that a fair price is not being offered.

9 Anderson (2017) also makes the point that Smith was writing at the beginning of the industrial revolution, before the belief, according to Anderson, that a free society of individuals could be built through a market society had been shattered.

10 Of course, there are markets that have asymmetries of information that may favour the buyer rather than the seller (e.g. some insurance markets). Also, the competitive market over even simple goods may incentivise market failures that are not easy to observe directly. For example, in an effort to keep prices down, the supplier of meat might source his product from farmers who house their livestock in overcrowded and unsanitary conditions, or may use artificial stimulants to maximise the quantity of meat available per unit of cost, etc. These practices could impose negative externalities on animals and harms upon consumers.

11 State-managed health and social insurance takes us into the realm of public rather than private decision-making, which will be the focus of Chapter 8. Incidentally, it is often said that egoism underpins the proper functioning of the private market mechanism, but as noted in Chapters 3 and 5 many liberals, although favouring market competition, reject the notion that humans should be, and necessarily are, driven by egoism. As a further example of the anti-egoist sentiment in liberalism, von Mises (1927/2005, p.14) maintained that

> the sacrifice that [society] imposes is only a provisional one: the renunciation of an immediate and relatively minor advantage in exchange for a much greater ultimate benefit. The continued existence of society as the association of persons working in cooperation and sharing a common way of life is in the interest of every individual. Whoever gives up a momentary advantage in order to avoid imperilling the continued existence of society is sacrificing a lesser gain for a greater one.

12 Still others may contend that the temptation to exploit informational asymmetries and the behavioural influences will be present in the absence of competition. That may be true, but again the counterargument is that competition, rather than being a force that drives out those temptations, serves as an additional incentive to act upon them, as one resorts to any means by which to prevent the loss of customers to one's business rivals.

13 One could argue that if a person decides to supply a particular product or service, then existing suppliers are harmed due to the potential for them to lose customers to the new entrant. However, so long as the new entrant is upholding the principle of a free and fair exchange, then the benefits to his new customers may well outweigh the harms to the existing suppliers, and the existing suppliers remain free to improve their own product or service (or to lower their prices) so as to prevent the erosion of their customer base. If they cannot provide quality and/or prices that match the new entrant, then they are, in effect, harming (or insufficiently benefiting) their own customers.

14 The behavioural scientist Drazen Prelec (2013) suggests that people attach what he calls diagnostic utility to the type of society in which they wish to live, which might mean that an intervention that, narrowly defined, represents poor value for money is valued highly because a failure to implement the intervention would generate considerable diagnostic disutility. For example, if a child were trapped down a well, it may cost a considerable amount of money to free him, to the point where, in relation to normal public investment rules, it would not represent good value for money to attempt to do so (exactly such a case occurred in Morocco close to the time of writing this note). But most people would likely consider it a very poor reflection of their society if the child were abandoned on that basis. My argument differs somewhat from Prelec's as I do not appeal to any form of utility as a justification for doing or not doing things, but the sentiment that people care about the general values that their society embraces is similar.

15 Of course, the generosity or otherwise of one's employer may depend upon one's occupation, a likelihood that I imagine neither Anderson nor Akerlof would contest.

16 The awards should, however, have some tangible value to the employees; otherwise, one might argue that employers are engaging in acts of exploitative manipulation.

17 In the Introduction to *Between Meals* by A. J. Liebling, the novelist James Salter (1986, p.xvi) wrote:

> There is still a restaurant Sorg in Strasbourg and it retains a star in the Michelin, a book Liebling held in disdain, not for any inaccuracy or lack of standards but because it is a symbol of the age of the automobile and the decline, in his view, of provincial restaurants in France. This may seem to be a contradiction but the speed and ease of car travel has meant that restaurants which once depended on a steady, discriminating clientele of business travelers now need only cater to customers who come once and are unlikely to return, at least for some time. As a result, the restaurants rarely change their menus and are not pressed to satisfy unfailingly, cook seasonal specialties, or try new dishes. A kind of anonymous patronage, such as one might find in a shoeshine parlor, leads to a lower level of art.

The message of this passage might be that for the benefit of all parties to an exchange, regular interactions, if at all possible, should be nurtured and cherished (NB. Sorg closed for good in the 1990s).

18 Reputational indicators are particularly useful when one does not know, or cannot even directly see, one's exchange partner. For example, think of the rating systems used on trading sites such as eBay, Amazon, Airbnb, etc. Unfortunately, it might sometimes be the case that suppliers treat their employees less than admirably in order to secure high customer rating scores, a point that re-emphasises the arguments made by Anderson (2017), summarised earlier. Different domains of mutual exchange – e.g. employer– employee, buyer–seller – may thus come into conflict with each other.

19 Specifically, the message read: 'If you needed an organ transplant, would you have one? If so please help others.'

CHAPTER 8

1 As argued in Chapter 1, the scarcity or abundance of the resources that we require in order to survive also direct the basic motivations that we choose or are forced to act upon.

2 There are parallels here with the economist Richard Musgrave's (1957, 1959) view that there are some goods and services – that he called "merit goods" – that should be given to people in kind, due to the benefit that they offer, rather than be distributed according to ability to pay. The delivery of

merit goods is usually justified on both internality (i.e. that they are otherwise underconsumed due to information failures) and externality (i.e. that they generate broader societal benefits beyond the direct consumer) grounds. The focus of the justification for public sector services in my political economy of behavioural public policy has a slightly different nuance – i.e. as already stated, that they give everyone (and thus not just a minority of the population) access to "conditions" (health, knowledge) that may be necessary for them to pursue their own notion of a desired life – and is thus conceptually closer to Sen's capabilities and Rawls's primary goods.

3 Mill (1848/1970, p.346), in his *Principles of Political Economy*, wrote that: 'Government aid, when given merely in default of private enterprise, should be so given as to be as far as possible a course of education for the people in the art of accomplishing great objects by individual energy and voluntary co-operation.' This appears to be Mill's method of nourishing flourishing.

4 Unlike utility maximisation, the collective public sector objectives do not constitute a view from nowhere. They are goals specific to the policy sector in question and, where they exist, were generally and broadly agreed upon.

5 Or more accurately, the earlier discussion echoes Mill rather than vice versa. In these views, Mill did not limit himself to education. For instance, he wrote that:

> In the particular circumstances of a given age or nation, there is scarcely anything really important to the general interest, which it may not be desirable, or even necessary, that the government should take upon itself, not because private individuals cannot effectually perform it, but because they will not. At some times and places, there will be no roads, docks, harbours, canals, works of irrigation, hospitals, schools, colleges, printing presses, unless the government establishes them; the public being either too poor to command the necessary resources, or too little advanced in intelligence to appreciate the ends, or not sufficiently practised in joint action to be capable of the means.
>
> (Mill, 1848/1970, p.345)

6 Musgrave (1959) expressed views similar to those of Mill on education; in essence, Mill suggested that education is a merit good.

7 Mill's views on education cited above were, however, published in his
Principles of Political Economy, which von Mises apparently admired.

8 As indicated already, von Mises seemed to have a somewhat restricted view
of what people's private goals are, which he referred to as their "inner life",
apparently reducing that to happiness and contentment. This is a reason
why he did not think that public education can help in the pursuit of private
aspiration (i.e. he thought that too much formal education would make
most people unhappy, which, in and of itself, is not an unreasonable
supposition). But the important point is that even though he is a member of
the relatively more laissez-faire wing of liberalism, he believed that there is
a role for government action in facilitating people in the private realm of
their decision-making. Moreover, von Mises is generally unsupportive of
government intervention to address negative externalities, and is thus at
odds with Mill's harm principle. It might also be worth noting that at face
value von Mises's (and the Austrian School's) view that liberalism ought to
focus on material well-being clashes with strands of nineteenth-century
French liberalism, which, according to Rosenblatt (2018), equated liberalism
to the pursuit of human perfectibility. That is, the latter placed great weight
not just on rights but also on duties – that a free man has a duty to improve
himself through the values of patriotism, dedication and self-sacrifice
(values that Mill believed gave people utility).

9 For a deep discussion of primary goods in relation to health and health
care, refer to the work of the philosopher Norman Daniels (1985).

10 Note, though, that von Mises (1927/2005), to name just one liberal, was in
principle supportive of government intervention to feed the hungry. The
selection of goods that are considered primary *and* are relevant targets for
government intervention is likely to depend upon time and place, because
the ability of all people to provide a good privately for themselves will
depend upon many factors, including wealth, the cost and price of the
goods/services in question, information and the extent to which people are
informed, culture and values, etc. Incidentally, Le Grand and New appear
to be challenging the notion that health care is a merit good, or at least any
more of a merit good than a service that provides food in kind.

11 Countries of course finance income support programmes via substantial
income redistribution. As discussed in Chapter 5, as part of a strategy to
nurture reciprocal instincts and, by extension, to promote human
flourishing, income and wealth redistribution from those at the top to "the

rest" ought to be far more pronounced in many countries than it has been in recent decades. The increased concentrations on income and wealth that have been witnessed are illiberal.

12 To offer the reader a reminder of what is meant by the collective action challenge with respect to a pure public good, consider the following passage from Weale (1978, pp.159–160):

> Hume pointed out that two neighbours may agree to drain a meadow which they possess in common, because each person can see that if he does not play his part in the project the whole scheme will collapse. By contrast, it is much more difficult for a thousand persons to come to a similar voluntary agreement, because, although the public benefit of having the meadow drained may be large, each individual's contribution to the social improvement may be small, and everyone will have a strong incentive to renege on his share of the cost of the project. However, the result of everyone acting in this individually rational way is that the project will not be completed and no one will enjoy the benefits of the social improvement. In situations of this sort, where the collective consequence of individually rational behaviour is a failure to provide a particular amenity or good, the state may non-paternalistically impose certain actions upon individuals for the other-regarding reason that the appropriate public good should be provided.

Although services such as health care and education are mostly not pure public goods because people can be excluded from their benefits if they do not pay for them, much of the population may be excluded from provision through a lack of means (and perhaps other factors) unless there is substantial cost-sharing. In order for the whole population to have reasonable opportunities to flourish in their private lives, the imposition of such cost-sharing so that publicly financed services for goods that are held as primary and that cannot reasonably be expected to be secured by everyone through private actions, is a similar non-paternalistic justification for government provision of those services. Admittedly, those who contribute to the costs of services used by others are perhaps, to a degree, harmed, but that is the price of securing a generally freer society.

13 The apparent exacerbation of food poverty even in some wealthy countries over recent years may cause many people to balk at this statement.

14 It may not necessarily be the case that greater relative country wealth leads to a greater demand for public services. For example, a very poor country may indeed warrant a National Food Service that in a wealthier country might not be deemed either needed or appropriate. Or in an extremely rich country with few poor people, a very even distribution of income and where the cost of services is modest in comparison to wealth, it might be decided that the provision of health or education services is best left to private actions. But, generally, wealthier countries will remain willing and are better able than poorer countries to extend and expand their range of publicly financed primary goods.

15 From a behaviouralist standpoint, Enthoven, an American free market economist, may not have been the ideal candidate to convince British health and social policy analysts, who typically lean firmly to the left of the political spectrum, on the best course of reform for perhaps the country's most cherished institution. Messages are most likely to persuade messagees when they trust the messenger.

16 Le Grand acknowledged that humans are driven by a range of different factors, including purely altruistic – or what he called knightly – motivations.

17 At the time of writing, Mackenzie Scott had recently donated $1.7 billion of her estimated $62 billion fortune to charity; she informed the world of that via Twitter. Perhaps she is trying to inspire other billionaires through a kind of indirect shaming to do something similar, but if she were motivated by pure altruism, why tell anyone?

18 Although I am arguing for a great deal of local autonomy over how public sector services are to be delivered, there will of course be responsibilities that liberals, such as myself (and Adam Smith – see Chapter 2), accept can only be concentrated within a central or national authority. The following from de Tocqueville (1835/1998, p.152), where he comments on the appropriate division of powers between the state and federal levels in the United States, illustrates this position (although I would warn also that the regions should not adopt paternalistic measures):

> The several states necessarily retained the right of regulating all purely local affairs. Moreover, these same states kept the rights of determining the civil and political competency of the citizens, of regulating the reciprocal relations of the members of the community, and of dispensing justice – rights which are general in their nature, but do not necessarily appertain to the national government. We have

seen that the government of the Union is invested with the power of acting in the name of the whole nation in those cases in which the nation has to appear as a single and undivided power; as, for instance, in foreign relations, and in offering common resistance to a common enemy; in short, in conducting those affairs which I have styled exclusively national . . .. The Union secures the independence and the greatness of the nation, which do not immediately affect private citizens; but the several states maintain the liberty, regulate the rights, protect the fortune, and secure the life and the whole future prosperity of every citizen.

19 I am of course aware that there are many prior and existing applications of reputational competition in both the public and private sectors, and have discussed some of them quite extensively in my previous writings. But the purpose of this chapter – and this book – is to propose policy directions that are allowable within the framework that I am proposing, rather than to review where and when applications have and have not worked.

20 One ought to be cautious here, however, because providers, who may have a better understanding of what is likely to improve the service than those who are intervening in their behaviours, might resist any perceived acts of manipulation or coercion (particularly if the reasoning behind such interventions is, in each case, not fully and explicitly explained to them), which is likely to damage their overall performance.

21 Heinrich (2021) may chastise me for claiming that most humans would accept these motivational characteristics, by arguing that their acceptance is dependent on culture.

CHAPTER 9

1 The threat of punishment, or negative reciprocity, will not, of course, deter all egoistic acts. Some egoists, who are sometimes called rational risk-takers, will estimate the potential benefits and costs of following their instincts and will act according to their calculations. Moreover, there will be other more impulsive egoists who continue to act egoistically whatever the potential costs and there will be still others who are simply unaware of the costs. However, the hope is that instituting punishment for transgressions will deter a sufficient amount of egoism to enable society to function effectively.

2 Von Mises's notion of happiness was apparently of the eudemonic kind. As noted in Chapter 8, he believed that inner happiness and peace of mind – which seems to align more closely with hedonic feelings – can only be secured internally by individuals themselves, and has no part to play in policy formation.

3 Von Mises's fellow Austrian School disciples Friedman and Friedman (1980/1990, p.22) doubted that advertising can manipulate people:

> What about the claim that consumers can be led by the nose by advertising? Our answer is that they can't – as numerous expensive advertising fiascos testify ... advertising is a cost of doing business, and the businessman wants to get the most for his money. Is it not more sensible to try to appeal to the real wants or desires of consumers that to try to manufacture artificial wants or desires? Surely it will generally be cheaper to sell them something that meets wants they already have than to create an artificial want.

One could counter that this is a naïve view of the power of advertising and its potential to manipulate consumers through the use of the behavioural influences, because many products may be wanted, if at all, in smaller numbers, *sans* advertising. Such (possibly deliberate) naivete among scholars who are associated with liberalism has probably provided ammunition for those who criticise the approach.

4 In *Utilitarianism*, Mill (1863/1969) maintained that punishment, retaliation and negative reciprocity in general have evolved to provide security, which he argued no person can do without, and he contended that security is a component of utility. I believe that providing security equates to protecting freedom, and people value freedom because it allows them to pursue their desires, which may, or may not, incorporate some notion of utility (see Chapter 4). Placing the utilitarianism to one side, however, there are many similarities between Mill's beliefs and the framework that I offer here.

5 This sentence resonates with the increasingly illiberal surroundings that many of us find ourselves in.

6 One could harm another party with the active use of the behavioural influences, but harms may also be imposed on another party if the behavioural influences cause one to be inactive. Both cases are legitimate grounds for potential regulation and the distinction will be considered in greater depth later in this chapter.

7 Some may contend quite legitimately that to claim that smokers impose no harms on others is an unreasonably strong assumption. For instance, there are possible negative externalities associated with passive smoking, and smokers may impose more costs upon health care systems than non-smokers (depending on whether the additional costs of smoking-related morbidity outweigh costs saved from earlier deaths). However, since the smokers themselves are not being manipulated to smoke, we cannot conclude that their behaviour is anything other than what they desire, and thus regulations imposed on reducing harms in this situation are tools not of behavioural public policy, but of public policy more broadly defined.

8 Producers of goods that are associated with significant harms are relatively highly incentivised to manipulate the exchange relationship as they may feel the need to counter the perception of those harms with more positive imagery and information pertaining to their products.

9 If we were to find that the person continues to smoke two packets of cigarettes in the absence of the attempted manipulation, then we may conclude that the intended infringement on a free and fair exchange had no effect. This of course assumes that previously used manipulation has no lagged effect when it is no longer used, which is admittedly a strong assumption, but if smoking rates do not fall, say, five years after a particular tactic has been regulated against (all else equal), we might decide that the tactic in question is, after all, harmless, and repeal any regulation against it. But if it is found not to work, there would appear to be no reason for the supplier of the good or service to start using that particular tactic again.

10 As a further illustrative example, in many countries a market in certain classes of drugs is of course illegal, but the total ban on trade in these products is motivated by policy that transcends behavioural public policy. The motivation for a complete ban tends to be the negative externalities that those who supply and consume these drugs impose upon society, as well as the harms that users impose upon themselves (perhaps with the justification that drug addicts lack full agency over their actions). If we based all regulation on behavioural public policy, it is unlikely that we would ban these drugs entirely – i.e. personal, moderate, recreational, considered use where few harms are imposed on others would be allowable. In these circumstances, we would at most try to regulate against any manipulations in an exchange relationship in a legal market.

This is not to argue for or against a complete ban on all classes of drugs (it may well be that the externalities imposed on third parties are generally perceived to be large enough to justify a total ban) – it is merely to illustrate where the limits of my conception of behavioural-informed regulation lie.

11 Many people believe that nudges do not have to target internalities; that they can focus on externalities. Nudges, however, are applications of a form of soft paternalism, and thus, definitionally, they must focus on internalities. But I will leave this debate hanging.

12 Steers can be used to reinforce budges because budges will rarely be foolproof. For instance, a fine for littering could be considered a budge if it is assumed that people litter unthinkingly and insufficiently consider the implications of their actions (i.e. the fine is meant to counter present bias). However, in order to fine people for littering, a person with fine-imposing authority has to observe them in the act, which is of course often impossible (at least, not without creating the kind of society that few of us would wish to live in). Thus, the green footsteps steer may consolidate the intended effects of the fine.

13 To reiterate what will by now be obvious, unless we desire serious incapacity or even an early death, our health is a primary good on which the pursuit of our private desires relies. That said, people may legitimately pursue activities in their private lives that damage their health and shorten their lives because those activities are also consistent with the pursuit of their other desires (i.e. pursuing all of our desires may lead to a shorter, unhealthier life than if we place some of our desires to one side). However, accepting a needed organ is unlikely to be traded off against other desire-led considerations for most people. Changing the organ donor registration default may be a fairly costless way of widening the opportunity set for someone who would choose an organ (essentially, a primary good) if it was made available to him. Waiting for or being denied an organ can generally be considered a pure harm that a health care system, given sufficient available organs, might be able to address.

14 Changing the default for organ donor registration could be categorised as a steer if one makes the argument that a person, following a shift from opt-in to opt-out, can still choose not to be a donor if they so wish, and therefore his liberty has been preserved in that respect. The counterclaim, as indicated above, is that the person no longer has the opportunity to opt in

(or to opt out by doing nothing), and therefore even if he is aware that the default has been altered, his liberty has been impacted upon, legislation has likely been used and thus the intervention is somewhat harder than a steer. Admittedly, in delineating the different externality-driven frameworks from each other (and in delineating the different internality-driven frameworks from each other, and, indeed, in delineating the different externality-driven and internality-driven frameworks from each other), there are grey areas. It may also be worth acknowledging that changing the default might not significantly increase the supply of organs at the point that they are needed because next-of-kin consent is typically required irrespective of the default position that a country adopts, and thus even if a person is on an organ donor register this does not necessarily mean that his organs can be used. However, adopting a position that increases the number of people on the register seems a necessary first step in resolving the problem of shortages in the supply of organs. Incidentally, seeing a value in the act of choosing, Thaler and Sunstein (2008) are opposed to presumed consent in relation to organ donation, contending that people instead ought to be prompted to make a choice between registering, or not registering, as a potential donor.

15 To be clear, I am not advocating for any of the budges summarised in this section; I am merely describing examples of potential budges. Incidentally, Mill (1859/1969, p.96) wrote that 'the class of dealers in strong drinks, though interested in their abuse, are indispensably required for the sake of their legitimate use. The interest, however, of these dealers in promoting intemperance is a real evil, and justifies the State in imposing restrictions and requiring guarantees which, but for that justification, would be infringements of legitimate liberty.' Mill thus expresses the view that drinking alcohol is legitimate, but that those supplying it have an incentive to encourage its use to harmful levels, and thus regulations ought to be imposed on them. However, Mill's recommendation may transcend my behavioural public policy framework. A budge would regulate against a manipulation of the exchange relationship, and although the possible negative externalities of alcohol may strengthen the argument for restrictions being placed upon any manipulation, a budge in itself would not in this case go beyond correcting for the infraction upon a free and fair exchange. That is to say, if people still consumed large quantities of alcohol in the absence of undue manipulation, there would be no scope

for a budge intervention to reduce their consumption. Broader public policy may, however, regulate for lower consumption if it was concluded that the level of alcohol that people genuinely desire was imposing excessive harms on society. Mill's quote nonetheless leaves open the suggestion that people might be imposing excessive alcohol-related harms on themselves; if that is what Mill is suggesting then it somewhat undermines his position as an anti-paternalist in this domain.

16 At the time of writing, the blogpost can be viewed at: https://blog .moneysavingexpert.com/2020/09/martin-lewis–i-confess–i-did-a–decoy-effect–experiment-on-my/

17 Many of the behavioural influences were originally observed empirically by asking people to choose between simple lotteries (or gambles). See, for example, my *Origins* book.

18 Other topical budges at the time of writing might be to mandate the wearing of face masks and to enforce social distancing during a pandemic, if it is assumed that people, due to the behavioural influences, fail to engage sufficiently with these activities in a voluntary system, if the interventions are not substantively burdensome to people (such that their broadly defined costs outweigh their broadly defined benefits), and if the justification for these interventions focuses principally on the protection of others.

CHAPTER 10

1 The behavioural influences most likely evolved for good reasons, otherwise it is unlikely that they would have evolved at all. It is possible that in modern societies these influences lead some people to sometimes make suboptimal choices – for example, to save insufficiently for retirement. After all, our hunter-gatherer ancestors probably had more pressing concerns than their retirements decades into the future. That does not make, say, present bias a bad "tool" – you might have the best screwdriver in the world, but it would be unwise to wash your car with it. Unfortunately, we cannot discern for whom and in what circumstances the behavioural influences are inappropriately applied, and thus "blanket" manipulations or coercions are ill advised. As argued earlier in the book, for internality concerns, we ought to restrict ourselves to educating people about the behavioural influences and the consequences of their actions

and then leave their choices to them. If people are, for their own self-interest, using the behavioural influences to distort the choices of others such that they are essentially imposing harms on them, then that, of course, is a different story.

2 The latter is not considered in this book, but may include laws governing the rights of spouses and civil partners, divorce and inheritance laws, etc.

3 See Chater and Loewenstein (2022) for a recent discussion of how tackling profound policy challenges requires regulation rather than demand-side behavioural interventions.

References

Akerlof, G. 1982. Labor Contracts as Partial Gift Exchange. *Quarterly Journal of Economics* 97: 543–569.

Akerlof, G. A., and Shiller, R. J. 2015. *Phishing for Phools: The Economics of Manipulation and Deception.* Princeton, NJ: Princeton University Press.

Allais, M. 1953. Le comportement de l'homme rationnel devant le risque: critique des postulats et axiomes de l'ecole américaine. *Econometrica* 21: 503–546.

Anderson, E. 1993. *Value in Ethics and Economics.* Cambridge, MA: Harvard University Press.

Anderson, E. 2017. *Private Government: How Employers Rule Our Lives (and Why We Don't Talk about It).* Princeton, NJ: Princeton University Press.

Aristotle. 1980. *The Nicomachean Ethics.* Translated by David Ross (Oxford World's Classics). Oxford: Oxford University Press.

Arrow, K. 1972. Gifts and Exchanges. *Philosophy and Public Affairs* 1: 343–362.

Attenborough, D. 1979/2019. *Life on Earth.* London: William Collins.

Banfield, E. C. 1958. *The Moral Basis of a Backward Society.* New York, NY: The Free Press.

Behavioural Insights Team. 2013. *Applying Behavioural Insights to Organ Donation: Preliminary Results from a Randomised Controlled Trial.* London: Behavioural Insights Team.

Bellamy, E. 1888/1996. *Looking Backward.* New York, NY: Dover Publications Inc.

Benjamin, D., Cooper, K., Heffetz, O. and Kimball, M. 2020. Self-Reported Wellbeing Indicators Are a Valuable Complement to Traditional Economic Indicators but Are Not yet Ready to Compete with Them. *Behavioural Public Policy* 4: 198–209.

Bentham, J. 1781/1988. *The Principles of Morals and Legislation.* New York, NY: Prometheus Books.

Berlin, I. 1969. Introduction. In Mill, J. S. [1863/1969], *On Liberty and Utilitarianism.* Oxford: Oxford University Press, pp. vii–xxxix.

Bernheim, D. 2010. Behavioral Welfare Economics. *Panoeconomicus* 57: 123–151.

Bernheim, D. 2016. The Good, the Bad, and the Ugly: A Unified Approach to Behavioural Welfare Economics. *Journal of Benefit-Cost Analysis* 7: 1–57.

Binmore, K. 2005. Economic Man – Or Straw Man? *Behavioral and Brain Sciences* 28: 817–818.

Blau, P. M. 1964. *Exchange and Power in Social Life*. New York, NY: Wiley.

Boehm, C. 2012. *Moral Origins: The Evolution of Virtue, Altruism and Shame*. New York, NY: Basic Books.

Buchanan, J. M. 1979. *What Should Economists Do?* Indianapolis, IN: Liberty Press.

Caldwell, B. 2005. *Hayek's Challenge: An Intellectual Biography of F. A. Hayek*. Chicago, IL: The University of Chicago Press.

Camerer, C. F. 2003. *Behavioral Game Theory: Experiments in Strategic Interaction*. New York, NY: Russell Sage Foundation.

Camerer, C. F., and Loewenstein, G. 2003. Behavioral Economics: Past, Present, Future. In Camerer, C. F., Loewenstein, G. and Rabin, M. (eds.), *Advances in Behavioral Economics*. Princeton, NJ: Princeton University Press, pp. 3–51.

Camerer, C., and Thaler, R. 1995. Ultimatums, Dictators, and Manners. *Journal of Economic Perspectives* 9: 209–219.

Camerer, C., Issacharoff, S., Loewenstein, G., O'Donoghue, T. and Rabin, M. 2003. Regulation for Conservatives: Behavioral Economics and the Case for 'Asymmetric Paternalism'. *University of Pennsylvania Law Review* 1151: 1211–1254.

Carlsson, F., He, H. and Martinsson, P. 2013. Easy Come, Easy Go: The Role of Windfall Money in Lab and Field Experiments. *Experimental Economics* 16: 190–207.

Carter, G. G., and Wilkinson, G. S. 2013. Food Sharing in Vampire Bats: Reciprocal Help Predicts Donations More Than Relatedness or Harassment. *Proceedings of the Royal Society B* 280: 20122573.

Chater, N. 2022. What Is the Point of Behavioural Public Policy? A Contractarian Approach. *Behavioural Public Policy*, forthcoming.

Chater, N., and Loewenstein, G. F. 2022. The I-Frame and the S-Frame: How Focusing on the Individual-Level Solutions Has Led Behavioural Public Policy Astray. Available at SSRN: https://papers.ssrn.com/sol3/papers.cfm?abstract_id=4046264

Cherry, T. L., Frykblom, P. and Shogren, J. F. 2002. Hardnose the Dictator. *American Economic Review* 92: 1218–1221.

Conly, S. 2013. *Against Autonomy: Justifying Coercive Paternalism*. Cambridge: Cambridge University Press.

Daniels, N. 1985. *Just Health Care*. Cambridge: Cambridge University Press.

Darwin, C. 1879/2004. *The Descent of Man*. London: Penguin Classics.

de Tocqueville, A. 1835/1998. *Democracy in America*. Hertfordshire: Wordsworth Editions Limited.

de Waal, F. 2010. *The Age of Empathy: Nature's Lessons for a Kinder Society*. London: Souvenir Press.

Dworkin, G. 1972. Paternalism. *Monist* 56: 64–84.

Easterlin, R. A. 1974. Does Economic Growth Improve the Human Lot? Some Empirical Evidence. In David, P. A. and Reder, M. W. (eds.), *Nations and Households in Economic Growth*. New York, NY and London: Academic Press, pp. 89–125.

Egan, P. 1830/2006. *Boxiana*. Boston, MA: Elibron Classics.

Engel, C. 2011. Dictator Games: A Meta Study. *Experimental Economics* 14: 583–610.

Enthoven, A. C. 1985. *Reflections on the Management of the National Health Service*. London: Nuffield Provincial Hospitals Trust.

Falk, A., and Fischbacher, U. 2006. A Theory of Reciprocity. *Games and Economic Behavior* 54: 293–315.

Feinberg, J. 1970. *Doing & Deserving: Essays in the Theory of Responsibility*. Princeton, NJ: Princeton University Press.

Feinberg, J. 1986. *Harm to Self. Volume 3 of the Moral Limits to the Criminal Law*. Oxford: Oxford University Press.

Friedman, M., and Friedman, R. 1980/1990. *Free to Choose: A Personal Statement*. Orlando, FL: Harvest.

Frijters, P., Clark, A. E., Krekel, C. and Layard, R. 2020. A Happy Choice: Wellbeing as the Goal of Government. *Behavioural Public Policy* 4: 126–165.

Hamann K., Bender J. and Tomasello, M. 2013. Meritocratic Sharing Is Based on Collaboration in 3-Year-Olds. *Developmental Psychology* 50: 121–128.

Hausman, D. M. 2015. *Valuing Health: Well-Being, Freedom and Suffering*. Oxford: Oxford University Press.

Hayek, F. A. 1944/2001. *The Road to Serfdom*. Abingdon: Routledge Classics.

Heath, A. 1976. *Rational Choice and Exchange: A Critique of Exchange Theory*. Cambridge: Cambridge University Press.

Heinrich, J. 2021. *The Weirdest People in the World: How the West Became Psychologically Peculiar and Particularly Prosperous*. London: Penguin Books.

Helliwell, J. F. 2020. Three Questions about Happiness. *Behavioural Public Policy* 4: 177–187.

Henrich, J. 2016. *The Secret of Our Success: How Culture Is Driving Human Evolution, Domesticating Our Species and Making Us Smarter*. Princeton, NJ: Princeton University Press.

Henrich, J., Boyd, R., Bowles, S., et al. 2005. "Economic Man" in Cross-Cultural Perspective: Behavioral Experiments in 15 Small-Scale Societies. *Behavioral and Brain Sciences* 28: 795–855.

Hertwig, R. 2017. When to Consider Boosting: Some Rules for Policy-Makers. *Behavioural Public Policy* 1: 143–161.

Huber, J., Payne, J. W. and Puto, C. 1982. Adding Asymmetrically Dominated Alternatives: Violations of Regularity and the Similarity Hypothesis. *Journal of Consumer Research* 9: 90–98.

Hume, D. 1751/2018. An Enquiry Concerning the Principles of Morals. In Coventry, A., and Valls, A. (eds.), *David Hume on Morals, Politics, and Society*. New Haven, CT: Yale University Press, pp. 3–131.

Hume, D. 1777/2018. Essays and Treatises on Several Subjects. Printed as Essays, Moral, Political and Literary. In Coventry, A., and Valls, A. (eds.), *David Hume on Morals, Politics, and Society*. New Haven, CT: Yale University Press, pp. 132–238.

John, P. 2018. *How Far to Nudge? Assessing Behavioural Public Policy*. Cheltenham: Edward Elgar Publishing.

John, P., Cotterill, S., Moseley, A., Richardson, L., Smith, G., Stoker, G. and Wales, C. 2011. *Nudge, Nudge, Think, Think: Experimenting with Ways to Change Civic Behaviour*. London: Bloomsbury Academic.

Kahneman, D. 2011. *Thinking, Fast and Slow*. London: Allen Lane.

Kahneman, D., and Tversky, A. 1979. Prospect Theory: An Analysis of Decision under Risk. *Econometrica* 47: 263–292.

Kahneman, D., Wakker, P. P. and Sarin, R. 1997. Back to Bentham? Explorations of Expected Utility. *The Quarterly Journal of Economics* 112: 375–405.

Kanngiesser, P., and Warneken, F. 2012. Young Children Consider Merit When Sharing Resources with Others. *PLoS ONE* 7: e443979.

Kant, I. 1785/1981. *Grounding for the Metaphysics of Morals*. Translated by James Ellington. Indianapolis, IN: Hackett.

Kropotkin, P. 1902/2014. *Mutual Aid: A Factor in Evolution*. Seattle, WA: Createspace Independent Publishing Platform.

Layard, R. 2005. *Happiness: Lessons from a New Science*. London: Allen Lane.

Le Grand, J. 1991. *Equity and Choice: An Essay in Economics and Applied Philosophy*. New York, NY: Harper Collins Academic.

Le Grand, J. 1997. Knights, Knaves or Pawns? Human Behaviour and Social Policy. *Journal of Social Policy* 26: 149–169.

Le Grand, J., and New, B. 2015. *Government Paternalism: Nanny State or Helpful Friend*. Princeton, NJ: Princeton University Press.

March, J. G. 1974. The Technology of Foolishness. In Leavitt, H., Pinfield, L. and Webb, E. (eds.), *Organizations of the Future: Interaction with the External Environment*. New York, NY: Praeger, pp. 131–142.

Markowitz, H. 1952. The Utility of Wealth. *Journal of Political Economy* 60: 151–158.

Mauss, M. 1954. *The Gift: Forms and Functions of Exchange in Archaic Societies*. Glencoe, IL: The Free Press.

Meyer, R., and Kunreuther, H. 2017. *The Ostrich Paradox: Why We Underprepare for Disasters*. Philadelphia, PA: Wharton Digital Press.

Mill, J. S. 1848/1970. *Principles of Political Economy*. Middlesex: Pelican Classics.

Mill, J. S. 1859/1969. On Liberty. In *On Liberty and Utilitarianism*. Oxford: Oxford University Press, pp. 1–110.

Mill, J. S. 1863/1969. Utilitarianism. In *On Liberty and Utilitarianism*. Oxford: Oxford University Press, pp. 111–172.

Mishel, L., and Sabadish, N. 2013. *CEO Pay in 2012 Was Extraordinarily High Relative to Typical Workers and Other High Earners*. Washington, DC: Economic Policy Institute.

Moore, J., and Desmond, A. 2004. In Darwin, C. [1879/2004], *The Descent of Man*. London: Penguin Classics.

Musgrave, R. A. 1957. A Multiple Theory of Budget Determination. *Finanzarchiv* 17: 333–343.

Musgrave, R. A. 1959. *The Theory of Public Finance: A Study in Public Economy*. New York, NY: McGraw Hill.

Nagel, T. 1986. *The View from Nowhere*. Oxford: Oxford University Press.

Nakamura, R., Pechey, R., Suhrcke, M., Jebb, S. A. and Marteau, T. M. 2014. Sales Impact of Displaying Alcoholic and Non-alcoholic Beverages in End-of-Aisle Locations: An Observational Study. *Social Science & Medicine* 108: 68–73.

Nussbaum, M. C. 2013. *Creating Capabilities: The Human Development Approach*. Cambridge, MA: Harvard University Press.

Oliver, A. 2013. From Nudging to Budging: Using Behavioural Economics to Inform Public Sector Policy. *Journal of Social Policy* 42: 685–700.

Oliver, A. 2015. Nudging, Shoving and Budging: Behavioural Economic-Informed Policy. *Public Administration* 93: 700–714.

Oliver, A. 2017. *The Origins of Behavioural Public Policy*. Cambridge: Cambridge University Press.

Oliver, A. 2018. Your Money and Your Life: Risk Attitudes over Gains and Losses. *Journal of Risk and Uncertainty* 57: 29–50.

Oliver, A. 2019. *Reciprocity and the Art of Behavioural Public Policy*. Cambridge: Cambridge University Press.

Oliver, A. 2020. Reviving and Revising Economic Liberalism: An Examination in Relation to Private Decisions and Public Policy. *Journal of European Public Policy* 12: 1763–1780.

Oliver, A. 2022. If You've Earned It, You Deserve It: Ultimatums, with Lego. *Behavioural Public Policy*, forthcoming.

Ostrom, E. 1990. *Governing the Commons: The Evolution of Institutions for Collective Action*. New York, NY: Cambridge University Press.

Ostrom, E. 2000. Collective Action and the Evolution of Social Norms. *Journal of Economic Perspectives* 14: 137–158.

Oxfam, 2017. *An Economy for the 99%*. Oxford: Oxfam.

Oxoby, R. J., and Spraggon, J. 2008. Mine and Yours: Property Rights in Dictator Games. *Journal of Economic Behavior & Organization* 65: 703–713.

Pinker, S. 2018. *Enlightenment Now: The Case for Reason, Science, Humanism and Progress*. London: Allen Lane.

Prelec, D. 2013. Decision Analysis from a Neo-Calvinist Point of View. In Oliver, A. (ed.), *Behavioural Public Policy*. Cambridge: Cambridge University Press, pp. 216–227.

Rawls, J. 1999. *A Theory of Justice*. 2nd Revised Edition. Oxford: Oxford University Press.

Raz, J. 1986. *The Morality of Freedom*. Oxford: Oxford University Press.

Rebonato, R. 2012. *Taking Liberties: A Critical Examination of Libertarian Paternalism*. Basingstoke: Palgrave Macmillan.

Reijula, S., and Hertwig, R. 2022. Self-Nudging and the Citizen Architect. *Behavioural Public Policy* 6: 119–149.

Rizzo, M. J., and Whitman, G. 2020. *Escaping Paternalism: Rationality, Behavioural Economics, and Public Policy*. Cambridge: Cambridge University Press.

Rizzo, M. J., and Whitman, G. 2022. The Unsolved Hayekian Knowledge Problem in Behavioral Economics. *Behavioural Public Policy*, forthcoming.

Rosenblatt, H. 2018. *The Lost History of Liberalism: From Ancient Rome to the Twenty-First Century*. Princeton, NJ: Princeton University Press.

Roth, A. 1995. Bargaining Experiments. In Kagel, J., and Roth, A. (eds.), *Handbook of Experimental Economics*. Princeton, NJ: Princeton University Press, pp. 254–348.

Ruffle, B. 1998. More Is Better, But Fair Is Fair: Tipping in Dictator and Ultimatum Games. *Games and Economic Behavior* 23: 247–265.

Russell, B. 1946/1996. *History of Western Philosophy*. London: George Allen & Unwin Ltd.

Salter, J. 1986. Introduction. In Liebling, A. J. 1962/1986. *Between Meals: An Appetite for Paris*. New York, NY: North Point Press, pp. ix–xix.

Samuelson, P. 1963. A Fallacy of Large Numbers. *Scienta* 98: 108–113.

Sapolsky, R. 2017. *Behave: The Biology of Humans at Our Best and Worst*. London: Bodley Head.

Sen, A. 1985. *Commodities and Capabilities*. Amsterdam: North-Holland.

Sen, A. 1999. *Development as Freedom*. New York, NY: Random House.

Sidgwick, H. 1891. *The Elements of Politics*. London: Macmillan.

Simon, H. A. 1956. Rational Choice and the Structure of the Environment. *Psychological Review* 63: 129–138.

Smith, A. 1776/1999. *The Wealth of Nations*. London: Penguin Classics.

Smith, A. 1759/2009. *The Theory of Moral Sentiments*. London: Penguin Classics.

Starmans, C., Sheskin, M. and Bloom, P. 2017. Why People Prefer Unequal Societies. *Nature Human Behaviour* 1: 1–7.

Sugden, R. 2009. On Nudging. A Review of *Nudge: Improving Decisions about Health, Wealth and Happiness* by Richard H. Thaler and Cass R. Sunstein. *International Journal of the Economics of Business* 16: 365–373.

Sugden, R. 2018. *The Community of Advantage: A Behavioural Defence of the Liberal Tradition of Economics*. Oxford: Oxford University Press.

Sugden, R. 2022. How Hayekian Is Sunstein's Behavioral Economics? *Behavioural Public Policy*, forthcoming.

Sunstein, C. R. 2013. *Simpler*. New York: Simon & Schuster.

Sunstein, C. R. 2016. *The Ethics of Influence: Government in the Age of Behavioural Science*. Cambridge: Cambridge University Press.

Sunstein, C. R. 2019a. *On Freedom*. Princeton, NJ: Princeton University Press.

Sunstein, C. R. 2020. Behavioral Welfare Economics. *Journal of Benefit-Cost Analysis* 11: 196–220.

Sunstein, C. R. 2022a. Sludge Audits. *Behavioural Public Policy* 6: 654–673.

Sunstein, C. R. 2022b. Hayekian Behavioral Economics. *Behavioural Public Policy*, forthcoming.

Thaler, R. H. 2015. *Misbehaving: The Making of Behavioural Economics*. New York, NY: Penguin Random House.

Thaler, R. H., and Sunstein, C. R. 2003. Libertarian Paternalism. *The American Economic Review* 93: 175–179.

Thaler, R. H., and Sunstein, C. R. 2008. *Nudge: Improving Decisions about Health, Wealth and Happiness*. New Haven, CT: Yale University Press.

Titmuss, R. M. 1970/1997. *The Gift Relationship: From Human Blood to Social Policy*. New York, NY: The New Press.

Tversky, A., and Kahneman, D. 1992. Advances in Prospect Theory: Cumulative Representation of Uncertainty. *Journal of Risk and Uncertainty* 5: 297–323.

von Humboldt, W. 1791–1792/1993. *The Limits of State Action*. Indianapolis, IN: The Liberty Fund.

von Mises, L. 1927/2005. *Liberalism. The Classical Tradition*. Indianapolis, IN: The Liberty Fund.

von Neumann, J., and Morgenstern, O. 1944. *Theory of Games and Economic Behavior*. Princeton, NJ: Princeton University Press.

Weale, A. 1978. Paternalism and Social Policy. *Journal of Social Policy* 7: 157–172.

Wilkinson, G. S. 1984. Reciprocal Food Sharing in the Vampire Bat. *Nature* 308: 181–184.

Winch, D. 1970. Introduction. In Mill, J. S. 1848/1970. *Principles of Political Economy*. Middlesex: Pelican Classics.

Xiao, E., and Bicchieri, C. 2010. When Equality Trumps Reciprocity. *Journal of Economic Psychology* 31: 456–470.

Index

For EU product safety concerns, contact us at Calle de José Abascal, 56–1°,
28003 Madrid, Spain or eugpsr@cambridge.org.

www.ingramcontent.com/pod-product-compliance
Ingram Content Group UK Ltd.
Pitfield, Milton Keynes, MK11 3LW, UK
UKHW020353140625
459647UK00020B/2434